A Bradford Pal

A Bradford Pal

GEORGE WILLIAM BROADHEAD
1894–1980

Private No. 476 'C' Company
18th Battalion West Yorkshire Regiment

JOHN BROADHEAD

Published by Uniform
An imprint of Unicorn Publishing Group
5 Newburgh Street
London W1F 7RG

www.unicornpublishing.org

A catalogue record for this book is available from
the British Library

5 4 3 2 1

ISBN 978-1-911604-94-5

Cover design Unicorn Publishing Group
Typeset by Vivian@Bookscribe

Printed and bound in the UK

THE GENERAL

'Good-morning, good morning!' the General said
When we met him last week on our way to the line.
Now the soldiers he smiled at are most of 'em dead.
And we're cursing his staff for incompetent swine.
'He's a cheery old card,' grunted Harry to Jack
As they slogged up to Arras with rifle and pack.
But he did for them both by his plan of attack.

Siegfried Sassoon, April 1917

CONTENTS

LIST OF ILLUSTRATIONS

LIST OF MAPS

FOREWORD

The members of the Pals Battalions are perhaps amongst the most well-known of the millions of British men who fought in the Great War. The Bradford Pals, like the Leeds Pals, suffered great losses in the Battle of the Somme, which has become the most iconic battle of the war, in part because its first day, 1 July 1916, saw 57,470 casualties, the highest ever suffered by the British Army. Stories of the harsh conditions and high casualty rates of trench-fighters on the Western Front have come to dominate public memories of the war. But this book gives us a much fuller and richer picture of what life was a like for one member of the Bradford Pals.

Like many young men who joined the Yorkshire Pals Battalions, George Broadhead was a well-educated clerk in civilian life – skills which were used by the military authorities, as many pages of the Battalion War Diary are in his handwriting. Although the Bradford Pals suffered grievous losses both at the Somme and in the Battle of Arras, the most traumatic episode for George was when a stray shell destroyed the Orderly Room tent in 1917, killing three of his best friends. This was the only episode from the war that he passed down to his youngest son, John Broadhead, the book's author. The hundreds of thousands of British men who were killed during the war were not, as popular imagination would have it, all mown down while going 'over the top', but often suffered more arbitrary deaths, being in the wrong place at the wrong time. Whatever the circumstances of their deaths, however, the grief felt by both families and comrades cast long shadows over the post-war years.

George's experiences also show us that the war was an opportunity for frequent encounters with French civilians, whether for the occasional 'good feed' of 'steak and chips', as George put it in one diary entry, or for developing romantic relationships. Like many British soldiers, he married a French woman he met during the war, and after the Armistice worked for the Imperial War Graves Commission.

John Broadhead is to be congratulated for the painstaking research that has gone into this account of his father's war. The brief personal comments from George's diary and the War Diary entries are brought to life by the inclusion of other voices, images and explanations. The resulting book is a fascinating narrative that deepens our understanding of what it was like for one young man to go through four years of war.

Professor Alison S. Fell, University of Leeds

February 2019

Mark Cross, Borough Studio, Dewsbury.

George William Broadhead (1894–1980). George was the fifth child and eldest son of Armitage Broadhead. He was born in the mill town of Batley in West Yorkshire.

INTRODUCTION

This is the story of my father, George William Broadhead, and his part in the First World War. It is inspired by a diary he kept from December 1915 to December 1916 in which he describes his experience as a volunteer soldier serving with the 18th Battalion West Yorkshire Regiment, known as the Second Bradford Pals. He handed me the diary not long before his death in May 1980, saying: *'Here lad, you might be interested in this.'* I had no previous knowledge of its existence but, like many other ex-soldiers, he rarely talked about the war and I can only recall a few such occasions. The most striking was his account of his narrow escape in June 1917 when he left the Battalion Orderly Room tent shortly before it was hit by a German shell and his three best friends were killed. He also referred to being deafened by a shell at Vimy, a deafness which grew steadily worse in later life.

In appearance the diary is a fine, leather-bound book which has withstood the rigours of war and the test of time. The layout is unusual in that all the Sunday entries are together at the back of the diary, a complication added to by his use of the Cash Account pages, also at the back of the diary, for the daily entries for the period from 6 December 1915 to 31 December 1915.

A note in the diary reads:

> *This diary continues at the beginning of this book and in case it should get lost or misplaced please forward to Miss Lily Parker 68 'Westvale' Thornhill Road, Dewsbury, Yorkshire, England.*

Clearly, Lily was a friend of special importance.

The diary entries display my father's fine handwriting and are written in indelible pencil. Keeping diaries in the field was against army regulations, for fear that sensitive information might fall into the hands of the enemy and a remarkable feature of the diary is that plans of the attack on the Somme on 1 July 1916, which must have been of the greatest secrecy, are drawn on several pages at the back of the diary. That said, it was well-known that many officers and men of the new volunteer battalions, who had grown up and worked together, had scant regard for Regular Army rules and red tape. As well as the daily record and battle plans, the diary includes details of weapon parts and other minor matters.

I cannot say why my father kept his diary. There are the obvious reasons and it is interesting that he chose a close friend, Lily Parker, as the recipient, in case, as he euphemistically stated, it should be '*lost or misplaced*'. The prose is matter of fact, containing precise and accurate details of locations and events but he spares the reader the fine detail of the horrors he witnessed. Notably, he does not mention the execution for desertion in September 1916 of two members of his battalion, Privates Wild and Crimmins, an event which must have had enormous impact on the rest of the men. For all that, the reader can detect a subtle change of emphasis from the first part of the diary, which shows an enthusiasm and interest of being part of what many young men must have seen as a great adventure, to the closing months of 1916 when tiredness and disillusion permeates his account. By this time he had seen the loss of many of his friends and acquaintances and, as with many other front line soldiers, he would have been acutely aware that there would be no early end to the war.

The year covered by the diary falls into distinct phases. In December 1915, my father set sail for Egypt and served there until March 1916 when his battalion was sent to France in preparation for the Somme offensive. The battle itself forms an important part of the diary, as does the period from July to October 1916 when the battalion was re-equipped and served in the Béthune sector. He spent the last three months of 1916 on the Somme again, with his battalion, participating in the final stages of the battle before going on leave in time for Christmas.

Much has been written about the Pals battalions: how they were recruited, the composition of the battalions, and how they were deployed and used in the Great War. In this context the history of the Bradford Pals stands square with that of the other Pals battalions but I hope the reader will find that by shedding a spotlight on a single volunteer soldier, a deeper knowledge and understanding will be gained of how ordinary men fared during one of the most significant parts of twentieth-century British history. In telling George Broadhead's story, I have concentrated on the period covered by his diary but I have also provided accounts of his early life in Batley, the formation of the Bradford Pals (including his enlistment), the period from January 1917 to his discharge from the army on 21 June 1919, his post-war life in France working as a 'gardener clerk' with the Imperial War Graves Commission and, finally, his later life back in his home county, Yorkshire.

I have drawn on the vast store of literature and online information concerning the war, as well as official and private papers, reminiscences and local newspaper articles. The ability to read his diary alongside the Second Bradford Pals Battalion War Diary (WO95/2362/2) has been of the greatest value, enhanced by the knowledge that after the attack on 1 July he was *wanted for working in Orderly Room*'. Part of his new duties was assisting with the writing-up of daily entries in the Battalion War Diary and the comparison of his private diary notes with the 'official' version is of immense help in bringing his experiences to life and providing the military context which dominated the soldier's life.

Other Battalion War Diaries provide vital information about the units in which George served from January 1917 to June 1919 when he was demobilised. Of particular interest is the War Diary for the 16th Battalion The London Regiment, the unit to which he was posted following the disbandment of the Bradford Pals in February 1918. A full list of sources is given in the Appendix.

The writing of this book would not have been possible without the constant encouragement of my wife, Jo, and the help she has given in piecing together the results of many hours of research. The motivation to dig deeper into my father's wartime story came some twenty years ago when we paid a visit to the National Archives in Kew to read the original copy of the Second Bradford Pals Battalion War Diary. The recognition of my father's distinctive handwriting was a moment of great excitement which prompted further investigation into the history of the Bradford Pals and many visits of exploration to the battlefields of northern France. This book is the culmination of that effort.

I am also indebted to other family members and friends who provided advice and information, and I thank Thomas who willingly became my researcher.

I never tire of reading my father's diary but I am not at all sure what he would have made of this account of his life. I remember well his gruff, matter-of-fact way and he would not have wanted a fuss to be made of his war service. He would certainly have been surprised at the enduring public interest in the Great War as exemplified by the place it holds in school curricula, film and television productions, book releases and the centenary commemoration events held by the British, French and Belgium governments to remember those who fell. It was a privilege to provide the BBC with material from his diary for the television broadcast on 1 July 2016 and to be present at Thiepval to witness the vigil and the commemoration.

First and foremost, my father was a down to earth, practical person whose loyalty to family, friends and country came before any self-interest. He came from an age when outward shows of emotion were not encouraged in men but the exchange of letters with my mother during her two difficult pregnancies in 1943 and 1945 reveal a sensitive and optimistic person. So much more is known today about the effects of war on the health and well-being of ex-soldiers, and in recalling the war my father must have had many dark moments. I count myself fortunate that he was able to overcome these trials and to live a long, happy and healthy life with his children and grandchildren. I cling to the hope that he would have been secretly pleased and proud that after the passing of one hundred years his story lives on in this book as a testimony to the conditions and fears which thousands of ordinary soldiers endured, and his desire and determination to do his duty. It is the story of a very special person.

John Broadhead

1

EARLY LIFE, 1894–1914

Batley is a busy manufacturing town situated in the West Riding of Yorkshire. It is the birthplace of the Shoddy trade, to which industry it owes its importance. Thousands upon thousands of our fellow-men in this country have been respectably clad in garments made from cloth manufactured in this town from cast-off clothing, so that there are few places in the wide world more universally known than Batley.

BATLEY CO-OPERATIVE SOCIETY LTD: A BRIEF HISTORY 1867–1917, BY W.H. CHILDE, 1919

George William Broadhead was born at his parents' home in Halifax Road, Batley on 19 November 1894. He was the fifth child and first son of Armitage and Mary Ann Brandon (née Haslam) Broadhead, and one of eight children. The names George and William were those of his paternal and maternal grandfathers.

His family were employed in the local coal mining and textile industries. They had not travelled far. In 1715 John Broadhead, George's four times great-grandfather was born at the village of Kirkheaton, close to Huddersfield and only some 6 miles from Batley. His family were hand weavers and clothiers and they would have used the local packhorse routes to take their woollen cloth for sale at nearby markets. John Broadhead's son, Joseph, married Martha Richardson in Dewsbury in 1760. It is likely that Joseph was a regular user of the packhorse road from Kirkheaton to Dewsbury, which follows the ridge above the valleys of the rivers Colne and Calder, and it was there that he met Martha. New employment opportunities beckoned in Dewsbury and its twin town, Batley, where the Broadheads were to settle.

The Industrial Revolution spelled the end of hand weaving in the area and brought a mass movement of population from rural villages, such as Kirkheaton, to the mills of the rapidly expanding towns. A history of Batley published in 1860 refers to a population of 12,000 residents and states proudly:

Perhaps no place has made such rapid increase in the number of its inhabitants, in trade and commerce, in the size and splendour of its public buildings as Batley. It is now regarded as a town of vast wealth; and if its manners are not so refined as in some other places, they are at any rate recommended by sincerity and honesty. The people however are generally well informed and mentally active; the diffusion of education has opened to the operative population the means of acquiring information upon almost every topic of general, political and scientific importance.

Despite this new wealth and the claims of an educated population, living and working conditions in the new towns were harsh. Batley's new-found prosperity was based on the Shoddy trade, an innovative way of reclaiming used wool which had been invented by Benjamin Law, one of the town's mill owners. A Superintendent of Factories report to the Home Secretary in the 1830s describes the manufacturing process:

Shoddy cloth is made from old woollen rags torn into pieces by a powerful machine, reduced as far as possible to their original form of wool, mixed with flock and then worked up again into cloth for any purpose where coarse woollens are required. In the tearing up of these rags a great quantity of dust is produced so that, generally, persons standing three yards apart cannot very clearly distinguish one another.

Lung and other diseases were common and life expectancy was low. By the turn of the century Batley's population had tripled and it was said that sixty mill chimneys could be counted in the valley. The thick black smoke which belched from the mills obscured the view and gradually caused the sandstone buildings of the town to be covered in a patina of black soot.

The Broadheads found regular work in the mills and associated industries, such as sandstone quarrying and coal mining. In the 1911 census Armitage Broadhead's profession is given as a foreman rag grinder. Armitage worked at Fenton & Son's Springfield Mill in Batley Carr and was in charge of four rag-grinding machines. He lived a short walk from the mill with Mary Ann, who was a weaver before her marriage. Armitage had some education but Mary Ann, at the time of her marriage in 1883, was barely literate, as evidenced by her use of a cross in signing the register of marriages. Armitage was also prepared to allow his sixteen-year-old son, George, with

Armitage Broadhead (1862–1945). George's father, Armitage was born in Batley and employed as a foreman rag grinder in Fenton's Mill, Batley Carr. He married Mary Ann Brandon Haslam in 1883 and they had eight children. He was a keen sportsman and influential supporter of Batley cricket and rugby league clubs.

Mary Ann Brandon Broadhead (1864–1928).
Mary was born in Aston, Birmingham and
came from a family with Scottish and military
connections. Until her marriage to Armitage
Broadhead in 1883 she was employed as a
weaver in Staincliffe, Batley. Her older brother,
Tom Haslam, played rugby for Batley, Yorkshire
and England, and was a member of the first
'Lions' tour to Australia in 1888.

his impeccable handwriting, to complete the 1911 census form but took care to sign it over the crossed-out signature of his son.

Armitage and Mary Ann's children benefitted from the 1870 and 1880 Elementary Education Acts which made it compulsory for children between the ages of five and thirteen to attend a day school. In 1868 Batley had been granted its charter as an independent borough and the civic leaders, who were largely mill or colliery owners, took great pride in improving the new town's appearance and public amenities. The building of schools, hospitals, civic buildings and utility and transport concerns were in the forefront of this movement. In 1871 the Batley School Board was formed and the first Board School opened in 1872 at Purlwell. The school was a non-denominational school set up under the Elementary Education Act and it quickly gained a reputation for excellence. It was housed in a fine, stone building, which is still in use today as a school.

The Broadhead family lived close to Purlwell School and George started his education there in 1899. His younger and older siblings were pupils at Staincliffe Church of England School, a National School, which was also close by and which was founded by the parish church in 1869. There is no record of why Armitage and Mary Ann chose to send George to a different school but perhaps they felt that their first male child needed more independence and a greater challenge.

In the early stages of compulsory education many families struggled to balance school commitments with the need to send their children to work or to help with large families. Fees were paid until their abolition in 1891 and many parents believed that the family's business came before the school's needs. Poor living conditions meant that illnesses were common and the daily log for Staincliffe School kept by the Headmaster, Mr Crowe, refers to the problems of poor attendance and the serious nature of some of his pupils' ailments. The log has entries concerning the medical condition of Annie Broadhead, George's eldest sister, who was absent for three months with a chest complaint.

Elementary education at this time was noted for its strict discipline and learning by rote. The quality of teaching staff varied and salaries were less than those of the mill workers. Headteachers often had to employ pupil teachers aged between thirteen and eighteen, and corporal punishment was commonly used to keep order. Good handwriting was given great emphasis and the acquisition of this skill was to serve George well at work and in the army. At the turn of the century the majority of children left school by the age of twelve but a small number of the more able children were chosen for further education which was geared to providing the technical, engineering and administrative skills needed by local industry. In 1907 George moved to Heckmondwike Higher Grade School, which subsequently became Heckmondwike Grammar School. He took great pride in being chosen to stay on at school to the age of fourteen and having what he described as a good secondary education.

On leaving school in 1908, George Broadhead found work as a clerk in the office of Batley Corporation Gas Works, which was situated in the works at the edge of the town. He was the first of the family to take office work in contrast to his older sisters, Annie, Laura and Lizzie who worked as rag sorters and rag grinders in the local mills. Sadly, all three and their mother Mary Ann died within three years of each other in the late 1920s. As a junior clerk, George's duties would have involved the keeping of records of consumers and suppliers. No doubt this would have been a tedious task carried out under close supervision but would have instilled the disciplines of accuracy and neatness which were to stand him in good stead in later life. His reputation as a reliable worker led to promotion and, after a spell working in the Town Hall, by the time of his enlistment in the army in 1915 he was Head Clerk at the Corporation Electricity Works. The excellent handwriting and generally correct English displayed in his diary are evidence of the thoroughness of his education and the nature of his early employment.

There is little documentary evidence of how George spent his youth but family photographs show that he was a handsome, smartly dressed young man who must have had many admirers. Lily Parker, who is named in the diary, was clearly among the foremost of these. The 1911 Census shows Lily as a 'shop assistant' living in Dewsbury with her widowed mother and brother, Allen, and sisters, Carrie and Ivy. References in George's diary to attendance at church services and the use of Christ Church, Staincliffe for family baptisms and marriages indicate that he was a practising member of the Church of England.

George inherited his family's love of sport. Information from his father's obituary, published in the *Dewsbury Reporter* on 2 February 1945, states that Armitage was one of the oldest supporters of Batley Cricket, Athletic and Football Club. Armitage was noted for his remarkable knowledge of the club's history, having seen the great Dr W.G. Grace dismissed first ball when playing against a team of locals. His brother-in-law, Joseph Thomas Haslam (known as Tom), was a professional rugby player who played at full-back for Batley, Yorkshire and England. Tom was a member of the first Lions

Lily Parker (1895–1968). Lily, a twenty-year-old shop assistant from Dewsbury, was George's girlfriend when he enlisted in March 1915. A note in his diary asks that should the diary be 'lost or misplaced' it should be sent to Lily. She must have been greatly disappointed to hear of his marriage to a French girl in April 1918. Lily never married.

tour to Australia in 1888 prior to the game splitting in 1895 into the separate codes of League and Union. Tom's brother, Willie Haslam, was also well-known in cricket and football circles. The elder of George's two younger brothers, Tom, born in 1898, was named after his famous uncle.

George's passion was for cricket and football. At 5 ft 8 in, he was of average height for the time and had a strong physique. He played as a fast bowler for Staincliffe Cricket Club, his local team, and in the summer of 1914 played as a semi-professional for Great Horton Cricket Club in the Bradford League. Match reports in the *Bradford Telegraph* show him batting at number ten or eleven. He said in conversation that he was on the books of Bradford Park Avenue Football Club, which at that time was a successful Football League club. However, there is no extant record of how successful he was as a player. His diary entries for November 1916 record his enjoyment at playing football and rugby when the battalion was out of the front line. A knee injury in early 1916, which involved spells in military hospitals, might have been a legacy of his sporting endeavours. George's sporting interests drew him to the city of Bradford, which might account for his subsequent enlistment in the Bradford Pals. Batley lies between the cities of Leeds, Wakefield and Bradford, and transport links in the early twentieth century were excellent. In 1911 the UK's first trolleybus systems were started in Bradford and Leeds, and the availability of trains, trams and motor buses meant that transport services were frequent and affordable.

George was close to his younger brother, Tom, who was born in 1898 and in later life they were regular companions at sporting events. Tom saw service as a conscript in the 7th Battalion East Yorkshire Regiment, winning the Military Medal on 26 September 1918 in an attack on the German Hindenburg Line. The medal citation from his Company Commander reads:

COMPANY RUNNER

This man carried messages backwards and forwards between B.H.Q and the Company, continuously passing through heavy enemy barrage and Machine Gun fire. Showed great bravery all through, and by pushing forward with bombs etc, showed a fine example to other men when the Company was temporarily held up by an enemy strong point.

To complete the Broadhead family roll call, Charles Frederick (Fred), the youngest child, was born in 1904. In 1932 he married Irene Waller, the cousin of Horace Waller, a Private in the King's Own Yorkshire Light Infantry and an old boy of Batley Grammar School. Horace was awarded the Victoria Cross posthumously for his bravery in resisting a German attack on 10 April 191917 during the Battle of Arras. Fred served in the RAF during Second World War.

2

THE ONSET OF WAR AND THE FORMATION OF THE BRADFORD PALS

This should be a Battalion of Pals, a battalion in which friends from the same office will fight shoulder to shoulder for the honour of Britain and the credit of Liverpool. I do not attempt to minimise to you the hardships you will suffer, the risks you will run.

LORD DERBY COINED THE TERM 'PALS' IN A SPEECH TO VOLUNTEERS AT THE KING'S
REGIMENT LIVERPOOL HEADQUARTERS ON 28 AUGUST 1914

The weather in August 1914 was warm and dry, and film and photographs of the time show people enjoying their summer holidays and following their leisure pursuits. Surrey led the county cricket championship race with its prolific run scorer, Jack Hobbs, regarded by many as the world's leading batsman, heading the batting averages. The twenty-year-old George Broadhead plied his trade as a bowler in the Bradford Cricket League which Hobbs himself was to join before his conscription to the Royal Flying Corps in 1916.

In August 1914 the city of Bradford had a growing population of 300,000. The small eighteenth-century market town had seen a twenty-fold increase in population and had become the world centre of the wool manufacturing industry. Bradford mills were noted for the manufacture of fine worsted cloth used for high quality clothing. Built in 1873, Lister Mill in Manningham employed more than 10,000 workers and was the largest textile mill in the world. In the second half of the nineteenth century the town council was dominated by mill owners who were largely Liberal in persuasion but the balance of power shifted and in 1906 Bradford elected its first Labour MP, Fred Jowett. On the outbreak of war the council was evenly balanced between the three main parties.

Throughout July 1914, following the assassination in Sarajevo of Archduke Franz

Ferdinand of Austria on 28 June, the threat of war on the continent grew apace. The British government's hope was that by exercising its traditional skills of diplomacy, the balance of power in Europe could be maintained and a general conflict averted. Austria's rash declaration of war on Serbia on 28 July 1914, followed by the mobilisation of Russian, German and French armies made war inevitable and Britain's attempts to negotiate a diplomatic solution came to naught. Germany's violation of Belgium territory was the *casus belli* for Britain, reinforced by the Entente Cordiale with France, signed in 1904, which gave Britain a moral if not legal obligation to support her near neighbour. For the British people, the declaration of war against Germany made on Tuesday 4 August 1914 was sudden and unexpected. The previous day had been a Bank Holiday and the citizens of Bradford were looking forward to the following week when the mills shut for the annual week's holiday, known as Bowling Tide, and many of the city's residents encamped to their favourite resort, Morecambe.

From Nelson's day and earlier, British foreign and military policy had been based on the use of overwhelming naval power to protect the trade routes of the British Empire and other overseas interests. With the exception of the limited 'adventure' in the Crimea between 1853 and 1856, the British Army had not fought a large-scale European war since the time of Napoleon, and its primary role was to protect the colonies and to act as a police force at times of civil unrest, at home or abroad. Consequently, on the outbreak of war the army was small in size compared to those of the other major European powers. The Regular Army had a strength of approximately 250,000 professional soldiers (excluding ex-soldiers with a Reserve obligation) of which half were serving in the colonies. It was supported by another 250,000 largely part-time Territorial forces charged with Home Defence but with no obligation to serve abroad. It was clear to the government that a rapid expansion of the army was essential if Britain was to meet its commitments to its French and Russian allies.

Unlike many of his contemporaries who were convinced that the war would be over in a matter of months, Lord Kitchener, the Secretary of State for War, held the view that the conflict would be lengthy and costly. He correctly perceived that the new weapons of war, artillery and machine guns, backed by the industrial capacity of the major powers, would make it impossible for one side to overwhelm the other in a traditional war of manoeuvre. Large armies would be needed to fight a battle of attrition and Kitchener's first act on the outbreak of war was to launch a massive recruitment campaign aimed at enlisting half a million volunteers. On the fourth day of the war, morning newspapers carried an advertisement saying, 'Your King and Your Country Need You', and the response from the public was immediate, so much so that the authorities could not handle the flood of volunteers. The published terms of service contained in an accompanying poster stated that General Service would be for a period of three years, or until the war was concluded, and the age of enlistment was from eighteen to forty-one, although recruits could not be sent overseas until they were nineteen.

In Bradford the initial surge of volunteers was directed towards bringing the local Territorial Army units up to strength, and on 11 and 12 August the fully manned 6th Battalion West Yorkshire Regiment and its accompanying artillery battery left the city for training in camps in East Yorkshire. Across the country, the government faced the problem of dealing with a veritable army of enthusiastic but impatient would-be soldiers and a public that was clamouring for action. The War Office plainly had insufficient resources to deal with the task and, as a temporary measure, cities, towns and influential individuals were authorised to set up and fund 'Citizens' Army Leagues'. These bodies were charged with forming new infantry battalions and training and equipping them until such time as the army was ready to absorb them. The new units became known as 'Pals Battalions', a term coined by Lord Derby, a professional soldier and politician, who led the recruiting campaign. On 28 August 1914, in a speech at Liverpool he said:

We have got to see this through to the bitter end.... This should be a Battalion of Pals, a battalion in which friends from the same office will fight shoulder to shoulder for the honour of Britain and ... of Liverpool.

On 3 September 1914, Alderman John Arnold, the Lord Mayor of Bradford, called a meeting of the city's prominent businessmen and citizens to press for the formation of a Bradford Citizens Army League. The *Yorkshire Observer* quoted the Mayor as saying:

The League would push men into the recruiting office and form a commercial battalion in Bradford as had happened in Liverpool, Manchester and Birmingham. This war had been thrust upon us and what we have to do is look to our homes and defend the dignity of the Nation. I trust that Bradford will rise to the occasion.

His speech was greeted with loud applause and the meeting agreed unanimously that a League should be formed and that Bradford should seek permission from the War Office to form its own infantry battalion. An Executive Committee was formed to run the League, which consisted of what the *Bradford Telegraph* described as 'the great businessmen of the city'. Mill owners, bankers, MPs, knights of the realm and every other major interest in the city were represented, although the Labour MP, Fred Jowett, withheld his support.

The necessary funds to form the new battalion were forthcoming and recruiting commenced immediately, even though official War Office approval had not been given. After some delay and impatience from League members, War Office approval was given on 10 September to the formation of the 16th (Service) Battalion of The Prince of Wales's Own West Yorkshire Regiment, which was popularly known as the 'First Bradford Pals'. Within a week 400 men had registered for service, increasing to a thousand by the end of September. Standards in physique and intelligence were set high and many were turned away but the Recruiting Sergeants were often known to turn a blind eye to whether the volunteer met the minimum age limit of eighteen. Most of the recruits were under twenty-one years of age and many had been educated at the prestigious Bradford Grammar School. A full battalion's complement of 1,064, supposedly suitably qualified and fit recruits, was achieved by November 1914. The League had a deliberate aim of recruiting men who they thought were 'the right sort of men'. Twenty-two per cent of the new recruits were clerks or commercial travellers, echoing Lord Derby's Liverpool speech and his reference to office workers. Forty-seven per cent were skilled or semi-skilled workers and only 11 per cent were unskilled. The majority of the twenty-five officers came from the Bradford area and had either Regular Army or Territorial Army experience. The Commanding Officer of the First Pals was Lieutenant Colonel George Muller, a retired Colonel of the local Territorial force, the 6th Battalion West Yorkshire Regiment who was a Bradford businessman.

Two similar Pals battalions of the West Yorkshire Regiment (15th and 17th) were recruited in Leeds but an attempt by Mr W.C. Coates of the 'Clothiers Arms' in Bradford Road, Batley to form a Pals battalion for the men of Batley, Dewsbury, Heckmondwike and Ossett, the area known as the Heavy Woollen District, failed through lack of support. There was also a notable lack of interest in Pals battalions in Huddersfield and Halifax, which did not form their own units.

The initial training and equipping of the First Pals was haphazard. Uniforms and weapons had to be improvised and training carried out in the local parks. The men returned home at night to sleep and it was not until 14 January 1915 that, following a parade and inspection by the Mayor in the Town Hall Square, they marched out of Bradford to a newly built camp at Skipton. At the outset conditions at the camp were poor and much effort was expended on improving the facilities and preparing roads around the camp. It was some time before the daily routine of soldiering was established.

Following the formation of the First Bradford Pals, there was a marked reduction in the number of Bradfordians coming forward to volunteer. Nevertheless, the League felt there was still sufficient interest to fund and form a second battalion and on 29 January 1915 War Office Army Council approval was given for the formation of the 18th (Service) Battalion of the Prince of Wales's Own West Yorkshire Regiment, the 'Second Bradford Pals'. Attestation began on 18 February and an intensive recruiting campaign was launched throughout an expanded area of Bradford, including Keighley, Ilkley, Otley and Spen. The League reduced the required minimum expanded chest measurement, and various advertising and propaganda ploys were used, including cinema shows, public meetings, military displays and, most spectacularly, an illuminated tram car with over one thousand coloured lights displaying the message, 'Join Second Pals at once'.

The recruiting campaign was successful and no less than twenty members of the Bradford Police joined at the same time. They were led by their Drill Sergeant Harold Scott, formerly of the Coldstream Guards, whose voice was so loud that the other recruits said that his words of command could be heard in Wigan. George would have been fully aware of the campaign and on 15 March 1915, aged twenty, he enlisted in the Second Bradford Pals – Private, Number 476 'C' Company. Apart from the publicity campaign, there are many reasons that might have influenced his decision to enlist, ranging from patriotism to encouragement or even pressure from family, employer, colleagues and friends. The Chairman of Batley Borough Electricity Board where George now worked was known to be keen on young men enlisting to do their duty. There is no surviving family memory or record of why he volunteered at that time, nor any record of why he joined the Bradford Pals rather than the Leeds Pals or the King's Own Yorkshire Light Infantry, both of which recruited strongly in the Batley area. His membership of cricket and football clubs in the Bradford area might have been the link and many sportsmen did join the colours. These included well-known footballers, such as two Bradford City international footballers, Dickie Bond and Harold Walden, and also cricketers and boxers. It was not uncommon for several members of a team to join as one. Whatever George's motivation, the early part of his diary shows great commitment to the cause and excitement at the adventure on which he had embarked.

By the end of April the Second Pals had reached full strength and after a short spell at Bowling Park in Bradford, they moved to a new camp at Ripon to join up with the First Pals. The two battalions were incorporated into the 93rd Brigade of the 31st Division whose divisional badge was the intertwined white and red roses of Yorkshire and Lancashire, the counties from which most of the volunteer recruits came. Alongside them in 93rd Brigade were the 'Leeds Pals' (15th Battalion West Yorkshire Regiment) and the Durham Pals (18th Battalion Durham Light Infantry), making a total of some 4,000 men.

At Ripon the Bradford Pals were the first occupants of what became a major military training complex dwarfing the adjoining town. The men's time was spent on drill, route marches, trench-digging and weapons training. Some attempt was made to practise tactical movements at company, battalion and brigade level but this was rudimentary training when compared to the level of professionalism in the French and German armies. Nevertheless, the training gave the officers the opportunity to allocate men to specific roIes, such as assault troops, ration carriers, stretcher-bearers, signallers, caterers and transport. In George's case he kept his place in 'C' Company as one of the battalion's front line troops. An advantage of Ripon's location was that the men could make frequent returns to their homes, which George no doubt enjoyed.

93rd Brigade moved south to Fovant in Wiltshire in September 1915. On arrival, the men were re-equipped with the latest model of the army's standard rifle, the Lee-Enfield Short Rifle with 18-inch bayonet. This effective and robust weapon, which stayed in British Army service until 1957, had a high rate of fire and good accuracy. The Pals undertook intensive training on Salisbury Plain, including practice with the newly introduced Lewis light machine gun and the Mills bomb, a much improved hand grenade, which unlike previous grenades had a reliable fuse with a four-second delay. The men were also given training in trench digging and the construction of barbed wire defences. The expectation was for an early departure for France as reinforcements to make good the heavy losses at the Battle of Loos which ran from 25 September to 15 October, and in which there were 60,000 British casualties.

Any thoughts of an early departure for the trenches of France and Belgium were dispelled when in November the Brigade was issued with tropical uniforms, including pith helmets and on 6 December 1915 the Brigade received orders to move. Private Fred Rawnsley of the First Pals said in later conversation:

> We must have looked a comical lot in pith helmets. We'd all got gas helmets, everything ready for going to France and we just had to hand them in and just go.

The Second Pals transport section, comprising 105 men, fifty-seven mules and 116 horses, went by train to Devonport Docks for embarkation on the auxiliary transport ship *Shropshire*. The remainder of the battalion; twenty-eight officers led by Lieutenant Colonel Kennard, including Reverend E.O. Martin, the Wesleyan Chaplain, and the Canadian Medical Officer, Dr George Boyd McTavish, plus 893 men, entrained for Liverpool docks. The overseas destination was kept secret from the men.

3

PASSAGE TO EGYPT,
6–21 DECEMBER 1915

Of course we have our dangers but we do not look at them in a serious light; coming here we missed going down to see the fishes by seconds only – more than once.

LETTER DATED 12 JANUARY 1916 FROM DR GEORGE BOYD MCTAVISH, MEDICAL OFFICER, 18TH WEST YORKSHIRE REGIMENT, TO A FRIEND

George started his diary with the following entries:

6 December 1915 – Left Fovant for Liverpool and embarked on the Empress of Britain. Spent the night on board in dock. Nearly 6,000 on board.

7 December 1915 – Left Liverpool for an unknown destination. Sleeping accommodation alright but grub rotten. Very little work to do except Physical Drill and Stand To for Grand Rounds.

The *Empress of Britain* was a 14,000-ton liner, built by Fairfield Shipbuilding of Govan in 1906. She was employed on the Canadian Pacific Line's trans-Atlantic route between Liverpool and Quebec. With an average speed of 18 knots she was the fastest ship on the route, making the crossing in just under six days. In 1914 the vessel was requisitioned by the Royal Navy and refitted with 120mm guns as an armed merchantman. The *Empress of Britain* operated in the South Atlantic and between Cape Finisterre and the Cape Verde Islands searching for German commerce raiders until May 1915 when she was re-commissioned as a troopship. In its peacetime role the ship had accommodation for 1,500 passengers. To fit it as a troopship, most of the cabins were removed and the open spaces were used to hang hammocks from the deckhead. Tables were provided below the

Empress of Britain. 'Awakened from afternoon sleep by a terrific crash quickly followed by another. Thought we were torpedoed but found it was our gun firing at two German submarines which were chasing us. Torpedoes missed us by about 30 yards.' The *Empress of Britain*, a former Canadian Pacific liner, left Liverpool on 7 December 1915 with more than 5,000 troops of 93rd Brigade aboard. After surviving a collision with a French transport and escaping the clutches of the German U-boats, she arrived safely in Port Said on 21 December 1915.

hammocks for the men to take their meals and additional toilet facilities were installed which proved to be totally inadequate for the large number of soldiers on board.

The *Empress of Britain* set sail at 10.00 am on 7 December with more than 5,000 men aboard, mostly from 93rd Brigade with some additional Army Service Corps men. The ship was seriously overcrowded, with lifeboats for less than 2,000 men. Enemy submarines were active in the Mediterranean along the route to their 'secret' destination, which they soon discovered was Egypt, and if the ship had been torpedoed, the loss of life would have great. The Battalion War Diary notes that there was an escort of two destroyers as the ship left Liverpool. The escort parted company with the *Empress of Britain* as she left British waters and from there she was expected to use her speed to avoid enemy submarines.

The accommodation on board was cramped and the food poor. On the fourth day at sea, George complained: *'Sickness very bad owing to sea being rough. Grub worse, life on board monotonous, no change in routine.'* C and D companies of the Second Pals were fortunate to have bunks but the rest of the soldiers had to use hammocks in the overcrowded spaces of the lower decks. The winter passage through the rough seas of the Bay of Biscay was a testing time for the troops and there was great relief on reaching Gibraltar to find warmer and calmer weather. George's diary entries for 11 and 12 December reflect the change in mood:

11 December 1915 – Everyone excited. Land seen for the first time since we left Liverpool (Morocco?). Spent the day cruising up and down near Gibraltar. Passed through the 'Straights' at night. Beautiful sight – excitement intense.

12 December 1915 – Speeding away to Malta – did 250 miles during the night. Sighting land and ships very regular and it is certainly not as monotonous. Sea calm and weather beautiful. North African coast in view.

At midnight on 13 December 1915 the ship collided with and sank the small French Auxiliary Transport, *Djingjurd*, which had sixty crew and passengers. The men took this serious event in their stride, as shown in George's report:

Sea still calm and weather lovely – climate mild – nothing unusual except a few ships. At midnight collided with a small Auxiliary Transport (French) which sank in a very short time. Crew numbering 63 saved with exception of Chief Engineer who was drowned. French ambassador's wife and maid (from Greece) on board. Both saved. Our ship was damaged but not serious. Behaviour fine. No excitement whatever. Chaps even refused to get out of bed.

Private Bell of the Leeds Pals said in a letter home:

For a moment the vessel rocked from side to side causing hundreds of enamel plates piled on the mess tables to slide to the deck adding to the alarming effect of the collision. The silence that followed was only broken by the shuffling of hundreds of men sliding out of their hammocks and feeling around for their life jackets in the almost complete darkness. After a short while our Company Commander addressed us: 'It's alright men, we have only run into a fishing smack.'

The Second Pals Battalion War Diary includes the 93rd Brigade Commander's commendation:

The GOC was very pleased with the conduct of the troops on board ship last evening and congratulates them on the steadiness they exhibited.

The *Empress of Britain* was delayed three days in Malta while repairs were carried out and the ship resupplied. The troops were impressed by the sights of Valetta harbour, the main base of the Royal Navy's Mediterranean Fleet. George recorded his impressions:

14 December 1915 – Arrived at Malta 4.45 pm and was very much surprised at size of place. Harbour simply wonderful and the natives very amusing. Spent the night rejoicing.

15 December 1915 – Unable to go on shore so was terribly disappointed. Watching boys diving for coins. Ships coaling so everything dirty. Harbour full of warships. Four magnificent French battleships, also four destroyers, two Torpedo Boat Destroyers and four submarines. The old HMS Terrible anchored 100 yards away. Three fine hospital ships in harbour. Talking to sailor from HMS Gloucester. Malta and Valetta are two most beautiful places and they certainly exceed anything which I expected. The place is of wonderful strength and would undoubtedly take a lot of forcing. The Emden's crew interned here. Band performing at night. Also captured German submarine brought in.

HMS *Gloucester* was a light cruiser built in 1909, and in June 1916 was present at the Battle of Jutland. The prisoners of war from the German light cruiser, *Emden*, were survivors of its sinking by the Australian Navy cruiser, HMAS *Sydney* in November 1914 at the Cocos Islands. The *Emden* had operated successfully as a commerce raider in the Indian Ocean, sinking more than twenty ships. The display of strength of the French Navy and the Royal Navy must have been a reassuring sight to the Pals.

The threat from German and Austrian submarines, operating from bases in the Adriatic and Constantinople, was a cause for great concern. In the spring of 1915 four large German Type 31 U-Boats entered the Mediterranean. Three of their commanders were to become the highest scoring U-Boat aces of the war and Kapitänleutnant Lothar von Arnauld de la Perière, who sank 195 ships, was the most successful submarine commander in history. The ocean-going Type 31s, known as the Pola Flotilla, operated from the Austrian naval base at Cattaro in Montenegro, which was perfectly positioned to intercept Allied shipping in the eastern Mediterranean. Each boat had a range of 9,000 nautical miles, had a surface speed of 16.4 knots and carried six torpedoes. Three of the boats were at sea when the *Empress of Britain* left Malta at 7.00 am on Friday 17 December for the final 1,000-mile leg of their journey to Alexandria.

During the afternoon of 18 December, George's afternoon nap was disturbed:

Awakened from afternoon sleep by a terrific crash quickly followed by another. Thought we were torpedoed but found it was our gun firing at two German submarines which were chasing us. Excitement intense. Went to bed and slept none the worse for the business. Torpedo missed us by about 30 yards.

Other men recorded the experience. Private Tim Wharton of the First Pals wrote:

It was common knowledge that we should have to keep our eyes skinned as enemy submarines were on the look-out for us and we were not long kept in doubt because the day after we left Malta one was sighted about 3.15 in the afternoon. Our ship's gun was immediately trained on it and we sent them a greeting in the shape of a shell which fell a little short. After a few minutes another put in an appearance, round went the gun and in a few seconds another shell was on its way. The fight between our gunner and the Captain of our ship and the submarine working for the chance to send 6,000 lives into eternity was one which left an everlasting impression on those privileged to witness it.

The Battalion War Diary reported somewhat prosaically:

Sighted submarine some miles off starboard. Fired 2 shots at her from ship's gun. Immediately afterwards sighted second submarine on port side, about 2,000 yds distant.

A letter from the Battalion Medical Officer, Dr McTavish to a friend is in a more light-hearted vein:

Of course we have our dangers but we do not look at them in a serious light; coming here we missed going down to see the fishes by seconds only – more than once.

The Pals could consider themselves fortunate in having escaped the clutches of some of Germany's best submarine commanders. During 1915 and 1916 more than 600 Allied ships, displacing over one million tons, were sunk by enemy submarines in the Mediterranean. RMS *Ivernia*, on which George and some of the Pals sailed to Marseilles in March 1916, was sunk by submarines on New Year's Day 1917 and the SS *Minneapolis*, on which the rest of the battalion sailed to France, was torpedoed on 23 March 1916, just two weeks after it had landed them in Marseilles. It was sunk by Kapitänleutnant von Arnauld de la Perière, captain of SM U-35.

The *Empress of Britain* carried on its way and Alexandria was sighted at 6.30 pm on 19 December. The journey to Egypt was the first time George had ventured abroad and for someone who had been brought up in the industrial north of England, the packed and colourful harbours of Valetta, Alexandria and Port Said were awe-inspiring. His diary entries record his impressions:

20 December 1915 – Alexandria looks fine from a sea view. Harbour packed with ships. Natives selling oranges etc from their small boats. American gunboat in harbour. Weather lovely but too hot, almost stifling. Left 'Alex' at 4.30 pm.

21 December 1915 – Arrived at Port Said 7.30 am. Wonderful sight going up the dock, almost every nationality represented in ships. 3 French, 4 British battleships in harbour. Finest scene we have yet beheld but not very happy because no money.

Arrival in an overseas active service zone before the end of 1915 entitled the Bradford Pals to the award of the 1914–15 Star. Their colleagues in 94th Brigade who arrived in the Canal Zone at the beginning of January 1916 were not awarded the medal, which rankled with the men for many years after. They felt that the journey through the perilous Mediterranean was active service enough.

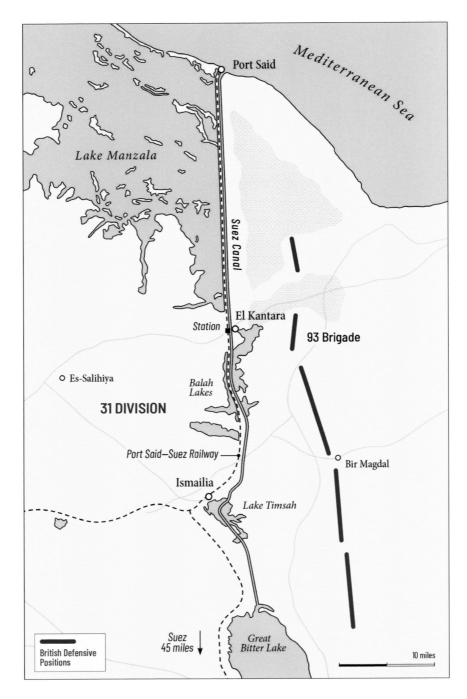

Port Said

Mediterranean Sea

Lake Manzala

Suez Canal

93 Brigade

El Kantara

Station

Es-Salihiya

Balah
Lakes

31 DIVISION

Port Said–Suez Railway

Bir Magdal

Ismailia

Lake Timsah

British Defensive
Positions

Suez
45 miles

Great
Bitter Lake

10 miles

Egypt – Suez Canal defences, 1916

4

EGYPT, 21 DECEMBER 1915–
10 MARCH 1916

You could not tell there was such an item as an enemy. If something doesn't happen soon this diary will not be worth reading.

FROM THE DIARY OF SERGEANT SAVILLE, 16TH WEST YORKSHIRE REGIMENT

Following disembarkation at Port Said on 21 December 1915, the men went into camp under canvas. There was relief at being back on firm land and George's diary entries for 22 and 23 December capture the first impressions of many men:

22 December 1915 – French seaplanes very busy flying around town. On land once more. Marched to camp at 9 am. Tents put up and once more soldiering. Biscuits and bully beef for meals and I am almost starving. Heat terrific. Went into Port Said at night. Surprised at European appearance of town. Almost imagined myself at home if not for the natives and their dress. No money so could not enjoy myself.

23 December 1915 – Camp. Bathing in afternoon. Went into town at night and had a decent time. Camp meals rotten – dog biscuits and bully.

The Battalion War Diary record of the arrival states that there were no casualties and the health of the troops was good, although one horse and five mules appear to have died on the auxiliary transport, *Shropshire*, which brought the battalion's baggage train and transport section. The men were also able to join up with friends for the first time since leaving Liverpool. George refers to meeting Willie Armitage, another member of the Second Pals. Willie was engaged to George's twenty-three-year-old sister, Lizzie (or Betty, as she is referred to in his diary) and they were to marry in 1917. George and

Willie were to be frequent companions as their wartime adventure progressed.

While the Pals were in camp outside Port Said, there was time for visits to the town but not without risk. On Christmas Day after attending a church service, George ventured into Port Said but found it: '*the vilest and most wicked place on God's earth*'. It seems he spurned the opportunity to attend a Christmas dinner laid on for 500 men and advertised in Brigade Orders, as follows:

On Xmas Day at 4 pm a Xmas Dinner will be served at the Casino Palace Hotel, and the Eastern Exchange Hotel, to be followed by a Grand Concert on the veranda of the Casino Palace Hotel. The bands of the 15th and 18th West Yorks will play selections during dinner, by kind permission of the Officers Commanding. Tickets for dinner may be obtained from the Battalion Orderly Room and the Weslyan Chaplain – price 2/6 each. Concert FREE.

On Boxing Day, while bathing, George was shocked by the sight of '*one of the 12th (Pioneers) Battalion KOYLI* [King's Own Yorkshire Light Infantry] *found drowned and with a dagger stuck in his back – murdered by Arabs*'. There was considerable Arab hostility to the British who were seen as an occupying power, and the Turks and their German allies were keen to foment unrest.

After ten days at Port Said, 93rd Brigade moved south to their front line positions near the town of El Kantara. The Pals battalions of 31st Division and its three brigades were part of the army's strategic reserve and their role in Egypt was to protect the Suez Canal from Turkish attacks. During 1915 the Turkish Army, supported by German military advisers, had occupied advanced positions in the Sinai desert and posed a serious threat to the safe passage of ships through the Suez Canal. The 100-mile long canal was a vital link in the sea routes from the East, which carried a large part of Britain's trade, vital oil supplies from Iran and troop reinforcements from India, and Egypt itself was the largest and most important British military base in the Middle East. The British government was understandably nervous about Turkish military capabilities, especially after the repulse of a major attack through Sinai in February 1915, which succeeded in reaching the canal and also the disastrous Gallipoli campaign, which concluded in December 1915. Urgent efforts were made to reinforce the canal's defences, and the task of 31st Division, which had a total strength of some 20,000 men, was to defend the northern part of the canal.

93rd Brigade was based on the eastern bank of the Suez Canal about 25 miles south of Port Said, near the railway station and small town of El Kantara which the Turks had destroyed in the February 1915 attack. George reported on his journey south and on his first sight of a war zone:

31 December 1915 – Left Port Said and had a good journey down the Suez Canal in a cattle truck. Lovely scenery. Arrived Kantara at 10 am and marched to camping ground. After dinner on fatigues so unable to look around.

1 January 1916 – Had a look at what was once Kantara before it was overwhelmed by Turks. Place a wreck and a most miserable shop it is. Nothing but trenches and wrecked buildings to be seen.

31st Division was not engaged in any serious combat during its stay in the desert, although George's diary includes reference to an action on 3 January when the '*KOYLI had a skirmish with Arabs and killed 48 out of 50. No casualties on our side.*' The men from the King's Own Yorkshire Light Infantry probably came from 12 Pioneer Battalion KOYLI, who were known as the Miners' Battalion. They were recruited in Leeds and provided front line assistance to 31st Division in trench-digging and other similar work. The skirmish is not mentioned in the memoirs of Captain R. Ede England, one of the battalion's officers, or in Battalion War Diaries, and there must be doubt about the veracity of the incident. That said, Arab irregulars who supported the Turks were active in the area and the British troops were understandingly nervous of contact with the tribesmen.

The Pals were engaged mainly in improving the canal's defences and training. Life in the tented camps at Port Said and El Kantara was notable for its lack of action, the cold and damp nights, and delays in receiving pay and letters. Egyptian climatic conditions were marked by intense heat during the day followed by bitterly cold nights and frequent sand storms. Scorching winds would arise without notice, which blew the sand with great force into every nook and cranny. Dr McTavish, the Battalion Medical Officer, made light of the conditions, describing them in a letter to a friend:

I've been real lucky and am Medical Officer for the nicest bunch of boys you could meet anywhere. I am having a fine time. You speak of hard work. Ha Ha! That was never one of my failings. Why it's only millionaires can visit Egypt and here I am getting paid to have a holiday. Nothing very hard about that.

Pay and letters took five weeks to catch up after the Pals departure from Liverpool, as George reported on 9 January 1916:

The day of all days – pay – first for five weeks. Happy once more. Letters arrived in the evening so happiness complete. Letters from cousin Gladys and Mother but was vastly disappointed to receive only a card from Lily.

Much of the eagerly anticipated mail had been lost when the P&O liner SS *Persia* was torpedoed off Crete on 30 December 1915 with the loss of more than 300 lives, so perhaps Lily might eventually have been forgiven. The *Persia* was one of the first passenger ships to be sunk in violation of internationally agreed Prize Rules which required submarines to give a warning to merchant ships and allow passengers to be evacuated before sinking the ship. The contravention of the rules by the U-boat commander, Kapitänleutnant Max Valentiner of SM U-38 caused considerable outrage as a number of American passengers were among the dead.

Army food was poor. The standard daily ration was 1lb meat, 1lb bread, 4oz bacon, ½lb vegetables, ¼lb potatoes plus some cheese and the means of making tea. Unfortunately, fresh meat and bread was rarely available in the desert and equivalent weights of biscuits and tinned beef ('bully beef') were substituted. The Huntley & Palmer biscuits had to be soaked in water, tea or gravy to make them edible and it was rumoured that some of the biscuits were old Boer War stock. The stay in Egypt was probably the first time the troops had experienced catering in the field in such difficult conditions and many of their letters home gave vent to their feelings about life in the desert.

As well as food, water supply was a problem and each man had to make do with just one water bottle a day for drinking and washing. The water was transported down the canal in small water-tank boats and was so heavily chlorinated it was barely drinkable. Men had to be warned from drinking from horse troughs, as the water contained dangerous bacteria. The 93rd Brigade order read:

Drinking water from horse troughs is strictly against orders and officers commanding units will in future deal with these cases very severely. All men are to be informed that drinking this water will produce Red Water Fever; which is in most cases fatal.

On 3 January 1916 George noted being put on guard over the freshwater tank, further indication that scarce supplies needed careful watching.

The Pals spent six weeks in their defence positions. The most frequent entries in George's diary during January and February 1916 are: *'nothing doing* and *same as usual'*. Sergeant Saville of the First Pals remarks in his diary: *'You could not tell that there was such an item as an enemy. If something doesn't happen soon this diary will not be worth reading.'* During rest periods, George took pleasure in meeting up with old friends and enjoyed meeting soldiers from other parts of the world. He tells of spending time with Indian soldiers of the Mysore Lancers who were part of 15th Cavalry Brigade and seeing Australian Engineers. The Brigade Gymkhana on 11 January provided some relief from guard duties and a *'fine display by Mysore Lancers – tent pegging, trick riding etc'* was much admired. During February he mentions his duties as Orderly Corporal, the first indication in his diary that he had been promoted.

There were a number of events during the month of February, which George found worthy of mention. On 4 February he reports: *'a fine monitor,* Sir John Picton *passed down canal about dinner time'*. HMS *Sir John Picton* was a coastal bombardment monitor with a displacement of 6,150 tons, carrying two 12-inch guns. She had been in action at Gallipoli, shelling Turkish positions and was now available to provide support to the army in Egypt. Three days later: *'German Taube aeroplane passed over Kantara but dropped no bombs. Turned back on reaching canal.'* Taube, meaning 'dove', was a German monoplane used widely during the first six months of the war. By 1916 it was obsolete and no longer in first-line service but the name was used frequently by the British troops to describe any type of enemy aeroplane. On 8 February the accidental death of two soldiers is recorded: *'Leeds (15th) man accidentally shot and killed. RAMC man also drowned'* and on the next day: *'Funeral of the two chaps who died. Very impressive scene. Our band played them to the graveside near number 5 post.'* The Leeds Pal from 15th Battalion West Yorkshire Regiment was Private Edward Wintle, aged twenty-one, from Ilkley. On 12 February, the Commanding Officer of the British troops in Egypt inspected the troops: *'General Maxwell and Staff visited Kantara and examined all the defences. Well satisfied with work done.*' General Sir John Grenfell Maxwell was to gain notoriety for the brutal suppression of the Easter Rising in Ireland in April and May 1916, including his somewhat arbitrary use of Martial Law and the firing squad to execute fifteen rebels in early May 1916.

On 18 February 1916 a persistent knee problem caused George to be admitted to 54th Casualty Clearing Station (CCS) for treatment. After the discomfort of tented accommodation in the desert he found it: *'very nice living but feeling uncomfortable with my knee in a splint'*. CCSs were located within easy reach of the front lines and were intended for short stay casualties. Longer or more intensive treatment usually involved a transfer to a General Base Hospital or Stationary Hospital, which would normally be located in a nearby town or city. Egypt was well provided with base hospitals and after four days in the CCS, George was transferred to 15th Stationary Hospital in Port Said where, in his words: *'slept in a proper bed once more'*. His diary entries refer to investigations into whether the injury was a displaced cartilage, cruciate ligament damage or chronic synovitis. On 24 February it was decided to operate:

> *Went into 31 General Hospital to be operated on for displaced cartilage. Finest hospital I have yet seen. 175 beds in one ward which was spotlessly clean.*

The hospital was located in a large converted warehouse on the western outskirts of the city and had treated many of the wounded from Gallipoli and the earlier fighting along the canal. Although the intention was to operate, the doctors decided that the ailment was cruciate ligament damage and surgery was not necessary, and that George should be transferred to the 'permanent base' where he would not be required to undertake front line service. When he heard that the Pals were to go to France, he pleaded with the medical staff that he should return to the battalion:

> *Heard that 31st Division were going to France so I appealed to the Doctor to let me go with them. Doctor saw the Major who after a bit of persuasion gave his consent to me going to France.*

He does not give the names of the doctor and Major but it is likely that they were Dr McTavish, the Battalion Medical Officer, and Major Johnson, the Battalion Second-in-

Command. On discharge from hospital on 3 March, he rejoined his battalion and '*was delighted to be with the boys once more. Went into Port Said at night ... had a real good time.*'

On 5 March 1916 he boarded the troopship RMS *Ivernia*, a 14,000-ton former Cunard White Star liner, with the parting words: '*said goodbye to Egypt and was not sorry*'. The voyage to Marseilles was less eventful than the passage to Egypt and was notable for '*splendid quarters – 2nd Class Berth*' and for the enjoyment of the '*simply magnificent*' sight of Sardinia as they sailed close to the coast. On 1 January 1917 the *Ivernia* became yet another victim of German U-Boats being sunk in the Aegean Sea with the loss of thirty-six crew and eighty-four soldiers of the Argyll and Sutherland Highlanders who were on their way to Alexandria to reinforce the army in Egypt.

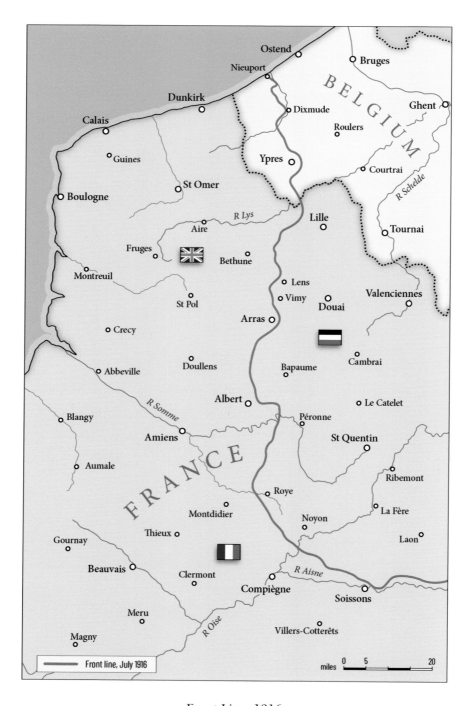

Front Line, 1916

5

FRANCE, 11 MARCH – 22 APRIL 1916

Little villages out of shell fire, some miles from the lines, were then of more use to us than Albert. Long after we are gone, perhaps stray English tourists, wandering in Picardy, will see names scratched in a barn, some mark or notice on a door, some sign post, some little line of graves.

THE OLD FRONT LINE, BY JOHN MASEFIELD, 1917

During the time the Bradford Pals were stationed in Egypt, a massive build-up of British troops in northern France had been underway. Kitchener's New Army now numbered more than half a million troops and, together with Regular Army formations, had largely replaced the French Army in Belgium and the Department of Picardy in northern France. Under the command of General Douglas Haig, the British Army held a continuous front of more than 100 miles stretching southwards from Ypres to the banks of the river Somme where it joined the French Army.

At the Allied Conference at Chantilly in December 1915 it had been agreed that if the enemy's strength was to be worn down, much better coordination of allied attacks on the various fronts was necessary. After much debate, an Anglo-French summer offensive on the Somme was settled upon with the Russians and Italians launching separate attacks on their fronts. Unfortunately, the Anglo-French part of the plan was disrupted by a surprise German attack on the strategically placed city of Verdun and its surrounding forts. The attack, starting on 21 February 1916 with unprecedented artillery support, had initial success and threatened to unhinge the French line and open the way to Paris. The French were forced to divert the bulk of their army reserves to Verdun's defence and the responsibility for the forthcoming Somme offensive fell mainly on the British. The arrival of the Bradford Pals in France on 11 March was part of the necessary build-up of troops.

The 600-mile rail journey from Marseilles to Pont Rémy, near Abbeville, some 40 miles behind the front lines, took 50 hours. Transport of troops was largely undertaken by dual-purpose wagons, marked '*quarante hommes ou huit chevaux*' – forty men or eight horses, not very comfortable but travelling at such a slow pace that the men had time to look at passing points of interest or even walk by the side of the train. Indeed, the average speed of 12 miles an hour was typical of journey times on the French rail system, which at that time was overburdened by military traffic and struggling with worn-out engines and rolling stock.

George's first impressions of France reflect the uncomfortable travelling and sleeping conditions:

11 March 1916 – Arrived at Marseilles 12 noon. Raining heavy at the time. Lovely place. Disembarked 6 pm and entrained in cattle trucks. Not a very comfortable night with about 30 in a truck.

12 March 1916 – Travelling through Valence region. Country magnificent and almost beyond description. Spent the finest Sunday that I can ever recollect although travelling accommodation not exceptionally brilliant. Passed French train loaded with wounded from Battle of Verdun. Pitiful sight.

13 March 1916 – Still in the train and scenery still lovely. Passed Paris (saw the Eiffel Tower) and Versailles. Saw the residence of the old French kings – beautiful. Arrived Pont Remy at 9.30 pm. Eight mile march to billets. Nearly killed me. Billeted in a barn.

14 March 1916 – Changed billets. Went into another barn with the lads. The village is a pretty place called Citerne. People here are farmers. Fine concert given by Leeds Pals in La Patronage Hall – an old barn.

By the spring of 1916 the British forces in northern France numbered more than one million and a vast network of military headquarters, supply depots, camps, hospitals and other facilities criss-crossed this part of France with major centres at Le Havre, Rouen, Abbeville, Étaples, Boulogne and Saint-Omer. Whilst it is widely recognised that the British supply and logistic system in France worked reasonably well, the rank and file infantry still had much 'foot slogging' to do.

The Pals spent twelve days at the small village of Citerne and were kept busy with drill, weapons training and twenty-mile route marches. On 25 March they set off on a forty-mile march to the front. This effort proved too much for George's knee and he spent the nights of 27 to 30 March in a military hospital at Beauval, some 15 miles behind the front line, where he complained of '*rotten grub and the usual monotony*'. On being discharged he had 9 miles to walk to rejoin the battalion at Beausart, a village within sound of the guns and his comment, '*the boys arrived late at night and like me were beat*', was written with meaning.

Proximity to the front provided a taste of what was to come. On 31 March George witnessed: '*an aeroplane duel – fine sight – German went back pretty sharp*'. But more ominously, on the next day, he saw: '*Colincamps bombarded and set on fire. Awful sight.*'

The battalion's home for the next three months was the nearby village of Bus-lès-Artois, one of the many small farming villages which dotted the rolling hills north of the river Somme and its tributary, the river Ancre. 'Bus', as it was known to the troops, was approximately 3 miles behind the front line and not far from the communication trenches which led to the battle zone. It was far enough from the front line to be safe from all but the longest range German artillery. The Pals were accommodated in wooden hutments and farm buildings which would be their place of rest following spells in the front line trenches and work for the engineers in the intricate network of support and communication trenches.

At this time the Second Bradford Pals underwent a change of command. On 16 April the Battalion War Diary reported the promotion of Captain H.F.G. Carter to Second-in-Command to replace Major Johnson, who was returned to the UK. Major Carter was to figure prominently in the battalion's actions and also, as will be seen later, George's military fortunes. Carter, aged thirty, was a professional officer of the King's Own Yorkshire Light Infantry who had won the Military Cross with 2nd Battalion KOYLI in October 1914 at Messines Ridge near Ypres. He came from a wealthy family with West Yorkshire connections and was one of the few army officers fluent in Russian and Japanese, languages he had acquired as a military attaché in those countries. His wife, Grace, came from the Guinness family. The following day, Major M.N. Kennard replaced his namesake, Lieutenant E.C.H. Kennard, who also returned to Britain. The thirty-four-year-old M.N. Kennard was also a professional soldier and his family's wealth from banking had helped him secure a place with 6th Dragoon Guards (Carabiniers), a prestigious cavalry regiment. Kennard had been wounded at Messines in October 1914, where he won the Military Cross. The Battalion War Diary does not give any reason for the new appointments but both men had combat experience in France and were much younger than their predecessors. The stresses of command in France often proved too much for older and less experienced officers, and General Headquarters was ruthless in returning them to Britain to fill training and administrative posts.

As it entered the combat zone, the battalion was at full strength, with twenty-eight officers and almost one thousand other ranks. There were four 'fighting' companies – 'A', 'B', 'C' and 'D' – each made up of 140 men and led by a Captain. George was in 'C' Company. Each company was divided into four platoons, commanded by a Lieutenant or Second Lieutenant, and with a mix of riflemen, bombers and Lewis Gun operators. The rest of the battalion consisted of headquarter staff, specialist trades ranging from shoemakers to medical staff, and those engaged in support tasks such as transport, ration-carrying, signalling, battle police and equipment salvage.

The first three weeks of April 1916 were spent in equipping and acclimatising the men for trench warfare. The battalion was given lectures on gas warfare and the men were sent through a gas chamber as practice. The Battalion War Diary refers to the provision of working parties to help with the construction of gun emplacements, trench repair and general fatigues. This clearly did not impress George, who ruefully commented that he was engaged for three days 'on fatigues, road sweeping etc'. His thirst for action was soon to be satisfied.

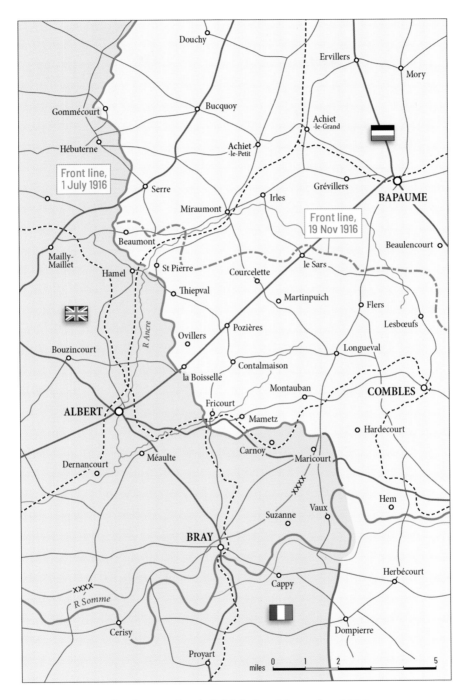

The Somme battlefield, July – November 1916

6

INTRODUCTION TO TRENCH WARFARE, 23 APRIL – 15 JUNE 1916

A while ago a blackbird spoke –
He didn't know the world's askew.
And yonder rifleman and I
Wait here behind the misty trees
To shoot the first man that goes by,
Our rifles ready on our knees.

FROM *THE LISTENING POST* BY ROBERT ERNEST VERNEDE, A SECOND LIEUTENANT
OF THE RIFLE BRIGADE. VERNEDE WAS WOUNDED ON THE SOMME IN 1916 AND
ON RETURN TO HIS UNIT WAS KILLED ON THE OPENING DAY OF THE BATTLE OF ARRAS.
HIS WAR POEMS WERE PUBLISHED BY HEINEMANN IN 1917

Planning and preparations for the summer offensive on the Somme were well advanced and reinforcement battalions were allocated specific parts of the front line from which they would launch their attack. The Somme was not the place General Haig would have chosen for the offensive; his preference was for an assault to the north in Flanders where a large part of the Germany army could be trapped against the coast, and vital ports, railheads and submarine bases captured. As the junior military partner in the Anglo-French coalition, Haig had to defer to Field Marshal Joseph Joffre, the French Commander, and agreed reluctantly that the Somme, where the two armies came together, should be the location for the joint British and French attack. In the event, the crisis at Verdun meant that only five French divisions could be added to the assault force of eighteen British infantry divisions from the Fourth Army commanded by the fifty-two-year-old Etonian General Sir Henry Rawlinson. Four cavalry divisions were held in reserve to exploit any breakthrough of the German lines. Rawlinson had his headquarters in a fine seventeenth-century chateau at Querrieu some 15 miles behind the front line.

The Somme landscape consists of rolling chalkland, dense woods and small, scattered villages. John Masefield, the Poet Laureate, visited the Somme in 1916 and wrote the following account of the battlefield:

The country north of the Somme is very like Wiltshire. The Somme and its northern tributary, the Ancre, cut deep valleys through the land, which runs in high irregular spurs down to the lower ground. Woods dot the hills and valleys, and on the spurs or sheltering in the re-entrants between them are a number of small villages.

Visitors to the area today will see little change. Despite the ravages of war which left the area a wasteland, the countryside gradually recovered and its appearance is now much the same as it was a little over one hundred years ago. The villages have not grown significantly in size and large farms, such as La Signy Farm and Rossignol Farm, still cultivate extensive sugar beet fields.

The deep strata of chalk which covers the Somme district meant that trenches and dugouts could be deep and well drained. Contemporary photographs taken by Royal Engineer surveyors clearly show the lines of German trenches caused by the chalk spoil which was used to create trench parapets. Later in the battle, when the ground had been torn by shellfire and bad weather was prevalent, mud became a serious problem. The Somme chalk, when mixed with a deep layer of loam topsoil, created a 'claggy' type of mud, which, glue-like, clung to everything it touched.

31st Division held the far left flank of the line of attack, opposite the small village of Serre. The division's front line stretched for just under a mile, running through a series of small copses growing along a bank. According to John Masefield:

In four places, the trees about this lynchet grow in clumps or copses, which our men called after the four Evangelists, John, Luke, Mark and Matthew. This bank marks the old English front line between the Point and Serre Road a mile to the south of it. Behind this English line are several small copses, on ground which very gently rises towards the crest of a plateau a mile to the west. In front of most of this part of our line, the ground rises towards the enemy trenches, so that one can see little to the front, but the slope up. The No Man's Land here is not green but as full of shell-holes and the ruin of battle as any piece of the field. Directly between Serre and the Matthew Copse, where the lines cross a rough lump of ground, the enemy parapet is whitish from the chalk. The whitish parapet makes the skyline to observers in the English line.

93rd Brigade held approximately 500 yards of the Division's front line, with no-man's land being no more than 100 yards wide. As described by Masefield, the Germans occupied the higher ground facing the Pals in a series of trenches crossing the fields in front of the village of Serre. The men of 169 Baden Infantry Regiment came from the southwest of Germany near the Rhine and Strasbourg. Unlike the British Army, the German Army's policy was to keep their units in the same part of the front so that they became familiar with the sector and its defensive needs. 169 Baden Infantry Regiment had held Serre since early 1915 and during that time had developed a formidable defensive system. The heavily fortified German front line was supported by a second line of trenches linked by communication trenches, with a third line of defence well to the rear and carefully concealed artillery of various calibres. Fields of barbed wire protected the trenches and there were strong points which projected from the front line, such as 'The Point' to the north and 'The Heidenkopf Redoubt' to the south. Concentrations of machine guns were positioned in the strong points and their overlapping fields of fire were able to enfilade the British first and second line of trenches and no-man's land. Crucially, the Germans had constructed a series of large reinforced dugouts in the front line and support trenches which were up to 30 feet deep and whose reinforced concrete and heavy wooden beams gave excellent protection to all but the heaviest artillery.

The Bradford Pals were introduced gradually to the art of trench warfare, with short spells of four or five days in the front line, alternating with similar periods in reserve in the support trenches and rest in their billets a few miles behind the lines. As well as acquiring experience of trench warfare and undertaking tactical training, the front line battalions were required to carry out extensive work for the engineers and also to move large quantities of ammunition and stores, both tasks being a necessary part of the preparations for the forthcoming offensive. Although there were benefits in gaining familiarisation with the trenches and their layout, this type of work was of questionable training value for assault troops and was dangerous, often being carried out at night and under fire as the men moved through the intricate network of trenches. The work of labouring was certainly unpopular with the men, and George described the engineers as '*pure and simple slave drivers*'. The Battalion War Diary gives a description of the type of work done for the engineers during April, which included opening up new trenches, widening, repairing, draining and cleaning old trenches, and repairing wired signal communication facilities which were often in a poor state due to damage from shelling and troop and store movement.

It was not until 23 April that the battalion had its first taste of trench warfare, having spent the previous six weeks training and labouring. On entering the trenches two soldiers of 'B' Company, Private G. Briggs and Private W. Barraclough were killed by artillery fire. They were the battalion's first combat fatalities on the Somme and are buried at the Sucrerie Military Cemetery close to the sugar beet processing factory near Colincamps, known to the men as the 'Sugary'.

The men's introduction to action was understandably a nervous one, as George's diary entries for 24 to 29 April reveal:

24 April 1916 – Entered the trenches at 11 am. Put in support trenches for first 24 hours. Artillery very active all day. On top all night digging. Absolutely tired out and jolly glad when we turned in. Two killed in 'B' Company.

25 April 1916 – Went into front line at dinner time so got a little sleep in the afternoon. On sentry during night looking over parapet. Very quiet night owing to working parties from both sides being out.

26 April 1916 – German artillery and trench mortars playing smash all day, although nothing landed in trench. Left the firing line at dinner time and put on guard over communication trench. Trench Mortar Battery causing its usual trouble. Bombarded German lines all day so Hun reciprocating with mortar bombs.

27 April 1916 – Whiz-bangs a speciality this morning. Trench Mortar Bombs absolutely a nuisance and causing us to be shelled. Hell let loose for an hour in afternoon and the Germans gave us souvenirs of all kinds. Shells bursting on parapet. Very quiet night except for plenty of rifle fire.

28 April 1916 – Bombardment by artillery of both sides simply terrific but the Huns seem to be suffering most. Anxiously awaiting relief which arrived late 5 pm so we left

Sucrerie Military Cemetery. 'Anxiously awaiting relief which arrived late 5 pm so we left trench 6 pm. Felt like entering a new world when we came out of the trench mouth at the Sugary.' The Sucrerie Military Cemetery was begun by French troops in 1915 and was used by the British when they took over the trenches opposite Serre village in late 1915. The cemetery (see above) was only a mile from the front and was named after the nearby sugar beet factory. The first two combat casualties of the Second Bradford Pals, Privates Briggs and Barraclough of 'B' Company, were buried there in April 1916.

trench 6 pm. Felt like entering a new world when we came out of the trench mouth at the 'Sugary'. Arrived Bertrancourt 8 pm.

29 April 1916 – Woke up still tired at 8.30 am and went to Bus for a bath and it seemed a treat after 4 days trench vermin. On and off parade all day and it was hard lines after the hard work we've done lately.

The Battalion War Diary contains accounts of officer led patrols whose task was to examine the barbed wire defences of both sides. Listening posts were also dug in no-man's land for the purpose of providing early warning of German attacks. In the course of this work an unusual find was made. The War Diary report for the night of 27 April states:

A listening post was established in disused trench running out from No 6 Post. The trench was blocked with wire and at the end was found the dead body of a man of the 9th Royal Irish Rifles. On being searched it was found that the man had two tunics. The outer one had been stripped of the buttons and shoulder straps but the under one had not been touched. Rifle (loaded 3 rounds), hat badge, private papers and identity disc sent Brigade HQ. Body was buried at Sucrerie.

It is possible that this unfortunate soldier was taking part in a patrol when he was killed. The use of a second tunic would appear to be an attempt to cover up his battalion's identity in the event he was captured by the enemy. The 9th RIR held this part of the trenches during February and March 1916.

During April the battalion lost eight men killed and eight wounded, all from artillery fire. These were not unusual casualty figures for routine spells in the front line trenches but George's account displays the reaction of raw troops who had not previously experienced the continuous threat of repeated shell and mortar fire. The underlying philosophy of the General Staff was for the army to be continuously on the attack and to harass the enemy as often as possible with artillery barrages, trench raids and nightly patrols of no-man's land. This of course prompted German retaliation and George was less than pleased to find himself at the receiving end of enemy shell fire following his own side's mortar attacks. The troops quickly learned to distinguish the different types of shell, and the reference to 'whiz-bangs' is likely to be to the standard German

77mm field artillery piece which fired a shell at high velocity, the whizzing noise of the travelling 16lb shell being followed by the bang of its discharge from the gun. The shell was particularly feared by the British troops as its speed allowed no time to take cover. The Battalion War Diary also refers to the enemy's frequent use of rifle grenades. The narrowness of no-man's land made these a potent weapon.

Bad weather inevitably made matters worse, as the trenches quickly filled with water and became very difficult to negotiate. Both sides struggled with the wet conditions and the Battalion War Diary entry for the night of 25 April reads:

> A great deal of work was observed being done by the enemy in front line trenches and support, baling and pumping going on throughout the day.

Further spells in the trenches followed in May and early June, interspersed with fatigues and drills, the most notable of the latter being on 10 May when, in George's words:

> Cleaning up all morning and on parade afternoon. Sir Douglas Haig and staff arrived and caught us drilling – passed us the compliment of being 'a fine smart body of men'.

As they went in and out of the line, the battalion suffered a steady stream of casualties, caused by sniping, shelling and the occasional trench raid. While repairing trenches on 16 May, George witnessed the death of a member of the First Bradford Pals:

> Went into trenches repairing. Sheffield Y&L suffered heavily – 60 casualties. Saw some terrible sights. One of the 16th (First Pals) caught by sniper – died just as we were passing him.

Private Willy Lassey is buried at the Sucrerie Military Cemetery.

The usual hazards of shelling had to be endured but some duties were more dangerous than others, such as on 23 and 24 May when George was on guard in exposed positions of the front line:

> 23 May 1916 – Went into firing line at 10 am and was put on Number 2 post (day post). Nothing happened during day. Terrific bombardment opened at 11 pm and continued for

three quarters of an hour – absolute hell. Bombing raid on our left and Leeds lost heavy but gave Germans a whacking.

24 May 1916 – Everything quiet again and spent day on look out – no casualties in our Company. Collared for listening post and spent the night in suspense. Pleased when brought out in morning.

Although the men were not necessarily in the front line, the repair work frequently exposed them to danger. George describes one such occasion:

31 May 1916 – Went digging at 7.30 am in support lines (Perry Street) converting old German trench into close support trench. Fritz spotted us coming in and shelled us all day so we had a pretty rotten time. Inspections when we arrived back, so this job a rotten one altogether.

It is most unlikely that George would have risked taking his diary into the front line and he probably kept it at his billet to be written up later. For example, his entry for 23 May records a particularly heavy German artillery barrage, which according to the Battalion War Diary occurred the following day. The writing up of several days' entries at a time would certainly account for any such discrepancy. Time at rest was more than welcome and during a spell in billets George enjoyed:

28 May 1916 – Cleaning up to look like soldiers again and had the usual inspections – gas bags, goggles, ammunition and rifles. Church parade in the old style and it felt a real treat. Jolly good sermon on do everything without grousing.

The period from 4–10 June was marked by heavy rain and George's diary entries for this period give a vivid description of the difficult and dangerous conditions:

4 June 1916 – Went into the trenches again with the battalion and 'C' Company occupied the reserve line. Carrying rations at night and it was a very heavy task.

5 June 1916 – Started raining so everything got messed up. Went up to the 'Sugaries' digging in the afternoon. Rationing at night and it was a bit awkward owing to rain.

6 June 1916 – Still raining and trenches getting into a bad state. Everything wet through and my feet are in a bad way. Ration carrying at night very bad and we were floundering all over the place. Heavy bombardment on, made things look worse.

7 June 1916 – Raining hard all day and trenches in a rotten condition. Digging in support trench all day and wet through again. Rationing at night was simply awful and it was up to the knees in some places in water. Fell in it twice.

8 June 1916 – At 10.30 am we relieved 'D' Company in the firing line and spent the day repairing part of the trench which a 6" shell had broken. The night passed quiet although it was terribly cold and raining once more.

9 June 1916 – Raining again and we are simply covered with mud, so all day we were trying to improve things by baling out. Our dugout has been blown in so we are without a home.

10 June 1916 – More rain and therefore more misery. Fritz playing the very devil all day. Put on listening post and soon after mounting got a couple of canister bombs over and very nearly blew us in. Very hot night. Fritz sent any amount of stuff over but did little damage. Sgt Green seriously wounded.

The twenty-seven-year-old Sergeant Harry Charles Green, died of his wounds in hospital on 22 June and is buried at Abbeville Communal Cemetery. Although the casualty list for this spell in the trenches was relatively light, with one killed and twelve wounded, the effect of this type of repetitive activity on morale is neatly captured by George's comment on 15 June:

Into the trenches again doing the old work, digging and like the rest I am about fed up of seeing these death traps.

As spring turned to summer, preparations for the offensive, or 'The Big Push' as it was popularly referred to, gathered momentum.

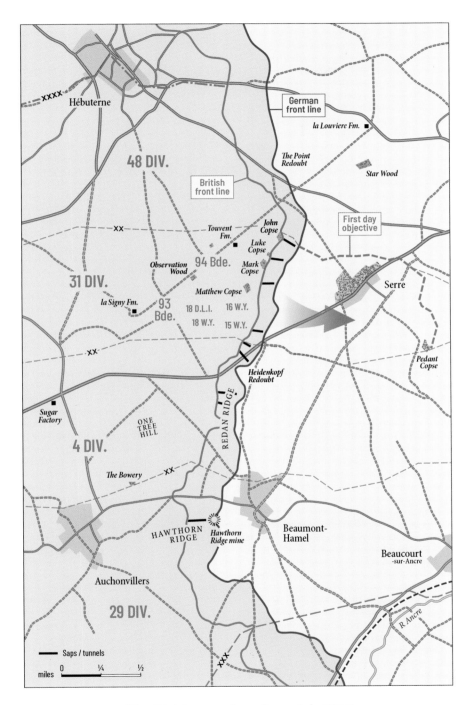

German front line

la Louviere Fm.

The Point
Redoubt

Star Wood

48 DIV.

British
front line

John
Copse

First day
objective

Touvent
Fm.

Luke
Copse

94 Bde.

Observation
Wood

Mark
Copse

Serre

31 DIV.

Matthew Copse

la Signy Fm.

93
Bde.

18 D.L.I.   16 W.Y.

18 W.Y.   15 W.Y.

Pedant
Copse

Heidenkopf
Redoubt

Sugar
Factory

REDAN RIDGE

ONE
TREE
HILL

4 DIV.

The Bowery

HAWTHORN RIDGE

Hawthorn
Ridge mine

Beaumont-
Hamel

Beaucourt
-sur-Ancre

Auchonvillers

29 DIV.

R. Ancre

Saps / tunnels

miles   0   ¼   ½

31st Division attack on Serre, July 1916

FOREST LODGE. LOGEAST WOOD

FORKED TREE . SERRE

SERRE

PINE APPLE SHAPED TREE

ROAD IN K. 30. c .

LEANING TREE. K 30.c. 97. E

Serre village, June 1916. This photograph was taken from the British front line by Royal Engineer surveyors. It shows the lines of German trenches in the field below the small village of Serre on the horizon. The village, which was some 500 yards from the British front line, was the 1 July objective for the Pals battalions of 93rd and 94th Brigades. The distance across no man's land was barely 100 yards.

Serre village, 2018. This was taken from the same position as the 1916 photograph above.

7

PREPARATIONS FOR THE ADVANCE,
16 – 30 JUNE 1916

The roads were packed with traffic. Column after column of lorries came pounding along bearing their freight of shells, trench mortar bombs, wire, stakes, sandbags, pipes and a thousand other articles essential for the offensive, so that great dumps of explosives and other materials arose in the green wayside places … the days of June were hard days for infantry who dug the 'leaping off' trenches and manned them afterwards through rain and raid and bombardment.

24 HOURS ON THE SOMME, BY EDWARD LIVING, PLATOON COMMANDER, THE LONDON REGIMENT, FIRST PUBLISHED 1918

The start of the Allied offensive on the Somme was heralded by a massive six-day artillery bombardment, the British contribution coming from 1,500 guns firing 1.5 million shells. The purpose of the barrage was to blow gaps in the wire and destroy the German trenches and dugouts so that the initial infantry assault by more than 100,000 men from fourteen British divisions and two French divisions could break through the three enemy defensive lines. Cavalry and more infantry divisions were in reserve, ready to exploit any breakthrough. Eleven of the British divisions were Kitchener New Army divisions, including 31st Division and the Bradford Pals who, as we have seen, were on the far left of the line opposite the small village of Serre. A mile to the north of them, two divisions of General Allenby's Third Army were to make a diversionary attack on the German defences in Gommecourt Wood. The troops of the French Sixth Army were positioned on the far right flank astride the river Somme.

The first direct reference to the offensive in George's diary is in the entries for 16–18 June:

16 June 1916 – was put on special ration party for the advance. Practising the attack all afternoon. Went down to the trenches carrying ammunition at night – awful hard work. Arrived back 4 am.

17 June 1916 – Fetched out of bed at 10 am to get ready for the trenches and went back carrying 60lb mortar bombs. Two journeys down to Matthew Copse to do, then finished.

18 June 1916 – Went down to trenches again 7 pm (Euston Dump) and was carrying rations down to Dunmow Street. Simply murder but got away at 1 pm tired out.

The army commanders were acutely aware that the volunteers of the New Army divisions were inexperienced and needed intensive training in mounting large-scale attacks, so that they had a good understanding of their objectives and could operate independently. Between 19 and 24 June, the Pals practised the attack at Gézaincourt, a village 2 miles to the south of the small market town of Doullens which was 12 miles west of the front line. George's account of this period gives a good insight into the nature of the training scheme and also the men's delight at being away from the front line:

19 June 1916 – Up at 9.30 am and was given the job of taking rations to Gézaincourt by bicycle and it was jolly hard riding a bike full pack. Arrived there 4 pm and it was a pretty little place – countryside glorious. Felt simply fine to be out of the sound of the guns. Saw a lot of French artillery.

20 June 1916 – Out at 7 am with a party under Major Carter and Captain Bakes putting out flags for the advance scheme. Spent a splendid day and one could hardly imagine that slaughter was being carried on 12 miles away. Battalion arrived here pm.

21 June 1916 – Battalion given the usual rest day. Inspections of everything. Went up to Doullens at night. Splendid place and it was delightful to see a town once more. Had a good feed into the bargain – steak and chips.

22 June 1916 – Practising the advance all day and was attached to the Stokes Gun. Had a decent day and got back to the village about 5 pm. Tired at night so didn't go far. Had

Gézaincourt. 'It was a pretty little place – countryside glorious. Felt simply fine to be out of the sound of the guns.' Gézaincourt, a small village close to Doullens, was where the Bradford Pals practised their attack on Serre in the days before 1 July 1916.

a good look around Gézaincourt – lovely place and inhabitants fine.

23 June 1916 – Same carry on – the advance. Got back early so went up to Doullens at night. Had a good time although everything is quiet.

24 June 1916 – Advance practice all day and still with Stokes gun. Had a very easy day so at night met Willie Armitage and went to Doullens with him. Had a good feed so perfectly satisfied.

25 June 1916 – Left Gézaincourt for Bus at 9 am and arrived rather tired at 2 pm. Great bombardment started but could hear very little down here.

On the back pages of George's diary are detailed sketches of the plan of attack. On arrival at Gézaincourt he refers to helping Major Carter, the battalion's Second-in-Command, with the positioning of coloured flags marking the phases of the attack and the layout of the German trenches around Serre. The men carried out repeated manoeuvres replicating the timing of each phase of the offensive. Each brigade and each battalion were allocated specific targets. 93rd and 94th Brigades were to lead the attack with the Hull Pals of 92nd Brigade held in reserve to exploit a breakthrough. In the 93rd Brigade sector the two Bradford Pals battalions were to follow the Leeds Pals in the initial assault with the Durham Pals held in close reserve. The attack was to start at 7.30 am and 93rd Brigade was expected to capture Serre within an hour and twenty minutes, and by 11 am reach the most distant objective, the 'Blue Line' which was the enemy's third line of defence. Although the 'Blue Line' was only just over a mile from the British front line, it would need a remarkable feat of arms to be reached.

The plans drawn on the pages of George's diary almost certainly come from the Gézaincourt exercise and a feature of the sketches is how closely they match the Army Corp's detailed plan of attack showing the enemy's trench lines and the timings for the capture of each objective.

Before leaving Gézaincourt, the men were addressed by the 31st Division Commanding Officer, Major General Wanless-O'Gowan. The fifty-year-old officer had the reputation for being a harsh disciplinarian, but he did have valuable active service experience from the fighting around Ypres in 1914 and 1915. He and the VIII Corps Commander,

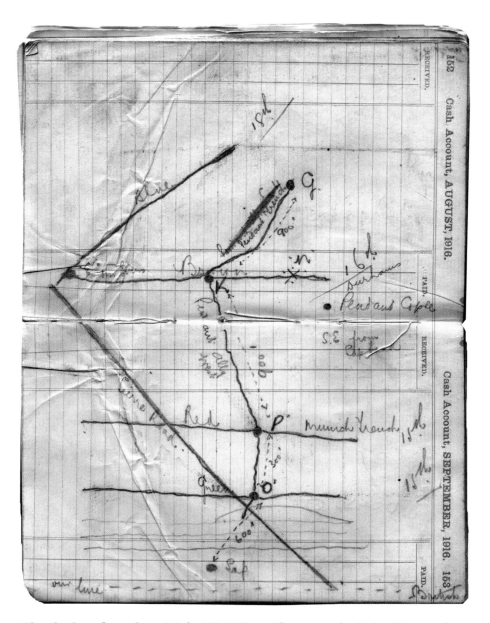

Sketch plan of attack on 1 July 1916. 'Out with party under Major Carter and Captain Bakes putting flags out for the advance scheme.' This sketch plan in George's diary was probably drawn during training at Gézaincourt in the period 20–24 June 1916 and would have been of the greatest secrecy.

Lieutenant General Sir A.G. Hunter-Weston, encouraged the men by saying that the artillery barrage was certain to destroy any enemy opposition and the men would be able to walk into Serre.

During the assault training at Gézaincourt, George commented that he had been attached to a Stokes Gun battery. The Stokes Gun, a 3-inch trench mortar firing a 10lb bomb, was the brilliant invention of Wilfred Stokes, the chairman of an Ipswich engineering company who offered the army his design of a simple tube mounted on an adjustable tripod. The cheap and easily produced weapon was rushed into service and at last gave the infantry the fire power and flexibility they needed for close support. The mortars were grouped in batteries under the command of the Brigade rather than the battalion. They were meant to play an important role in the attack giving close support to the advancing infantry with a 'hurricane bombardment' on the German front line.

On returning to Bus and the front line, George continued his Stokes Gun training and on 26 June was made orderly to Lieutenant Bobbie, the commander of Number 2 Battery. This changed, when two days later he was recalled to the battalion and was '*put on salvage instead of Stokes*'. His redeployment meant that he was no longer part of the assault troops who would 'go over the top' on the day of the battle. He does not say why he was moved to what was known as the 'salvage police' but as an experienced corporal with good organisational skills he might have caught the eye of Major Carter during the training scheme at Gézaincourt.

The 'Salvaged Stores' order written by Captain Williams, the Battalion Adjutant, lists the names of the four soldiers who would be based at Bus-lès-Artois under the direction of the Divisional Area Salvage Officer. The task of the salvage unit was to organise the recovery of discarded weapons, ammunition and other equipment following the attack. Rationing parties and other carriers returning from the front were expected to bring back as much as they could carry; not a pleasant task as some of the equipment would be on dead soldiers and the carriers themselves would be under enemy fire.

Another reason for George's reassignment might have been a last minute change of plan for the use of the Stokes Gun. Opposite Serre, nine shallow tunnels, called 'Russian Saps', some 10 to 15 feet deep, had been driven in great secrecy 100 yards forward of the British front line to a few yards short of the German line. The original plan, as shown in the Battalion Order for the attack, was that small mines would be exploded at the sap-head one hour ahead of the attack and Stokes Guns or machine guns would be placed in the craters to give protective fire to the troops as they crossed no-man's land. Although General Rawlinson, 4th Army Commander, had sanctioned the project for use across the frontage of the offensive, it was left to the individual divisional commanders to decide whether or not to use the tunnels. The 31st Division Commander, Major General Wanless-O'Gowan, was convinced that the German trenches would be destroyed by the massive artillery barrage and considered that the blowing and manning of the saps would be an unnecessary complication for his inexperienced troops. He decided that only one of the tunnels at Serre should be used, which meant that some of the Stokes Gun operators could be released for other duties.

Major Stokes, of the Royal Engineers, who was responsible for overseeing the construction of the saps, was highly critical of the failure to use this surprise weapon on the northern part of the battlefield. He believed that if all the saps had been used at Serre, 'capture of the front line at least would have been assured'. Because of the need for secrecy about the location of the tunnels, some of the battalion commanders were even unaware of their existence, although this does not seem to have been the case with the Bradford Pals.

The artillery barrage started on 25 June and although its noise and fury was an impressive affair, all did not go well in the days immediately before the attack. It had been intended to launch the infantry assault on 29 June but heavy thunderstorms on three consecutive nights caused a forty-eight-hour postponement. The delay unsettled the troops who, according to George, were 'vexed because they got drunk for the occasion'. Men in the front line trenches were allowed a rum ration of a third of a pint a week to be drunk at dawn and dusk, with extra rations should the men be about to 'go over the top' in an assault. The gallon rum jars were marked 'S.R.D', meaning Service Rations Depot but translated by the men as 'Seldom Reaches Destination'. On this occasion the ration might have been too liberal, perhaps not helped by those who were teetotal and willing to let their comrades have their share.

In an attempt to assess the damage to the German trenches caused by the bombardment, a raid on the enemy front line was launched on the night of 29 June. The Battalion War Diary states: 'Instructions were received from Brigade to make a raid on the enemy front line on night of 29/30 June. Three officers and Lieutenant McTavish, the battalion Medical Officer were taken to the trenches in motor lorries.' The report of Lieutenant Clough, who led the attack, is included in the Battalion War Diary:

Left our front line trenches as scheduled 12.28 am. Advance was slow owing to numerous shell holes and flares. Apparently our party was seen almost as soon as we had left our own trenches, for they seemed prepared for us and we were met by bombs when between 25 and 30 yards from their trenches. They sent up a single green rocket and formed a barrage of hand grenades in front of us and trench mortars and artillery behind us. The trenches seemed fairly knocked about, and the wire was cut where we were in sufficient quantity to allow the passage of troops. Their trenches seemed very full of men and apparently very deep. Finding we could not get forward, I brought my party back as well and as soon as possible as I could. As far as I can judge, my casualties at present are about 10 killed and 13 wounded out of 38 men and 4 officers. I have been slightly wounded myself in two places.

George's account bears out the failure of the raid:

29 June 1916 – Seeking chaps for big bombing raid and Joe Hodgson volunteered. Working in trenches all day and bombardment so terrific we couldn't make ourselves heard. Joe had left when I got back 8.30 pm.

30 June 2016 – Bombing raid last night an absolute failure. 29 casualties out of 40. Joe Hodgson missing.

Private Hodgson's name is on the Thiepval memorial to the missing. Two survivors, Sergeant Dyson and Private Waddington, were awarded the MM and DCM for their bravery in recovering wounded men. Both were killed the next day.

The meagre results of the raid should have given the generals and their staff considerable cause for concern, as the success of the forthcoming attack was crucially dependent on the destruction of the enemy positions. Other patrols on the VIII Corps front also reported that there were no gaps in the German wire and despite the battering they had received, it must have been clear that the enemy was alert and capable of mounting fierce resistance from their front line trenches and supporting artillery. Otto Lais of the 8 Baden Infantry Regiment 169 describes conditions in the German trenches:

Those of us whose dugouts had not been crushed, crouched below on the alert, took breaths, whether of smoke, dust or shell-bursts, gasping and with difficulty, believed by the third day that the unrelenting booming, rolling, cracking and bursting, on the top of the shaking and trembling of the earth, would drive us mad. On the sixth and seventh days the fury seemed to increase, the dugout entrances were mostly blocked leaving where it was going well, space to crawl through; the nerves of the occupiers were dulled, a suppressed rage lay in the tortured minds and souls of the defenders, one thought dominating all: 'when will they come?'

An indication of the stress which the British troops were under on the eve of battle was the desertion on the day before the attack of two men from the Second Bradford Pals. Privates Wild and Crimmins, who had been detailed to act as ration carriers during the attack, disobeyed orders to stay in camp and at lunchtime went to a local estaminet in Bus for a drink. Worse for wear, they failed to report for duty at the appointed time and were posted as absent. They were caught five days later by the Military Police, several miles behind the lines and were kept in custody before being returned to the battalion on 15 July. According to witnesses, it seems that the men did not fully appreciate the seriousness of their offence or the likely consequences. After a spell in the battalion guardroom they returned to front line duty on 27 July while awaiting their fate before the inevitable court martial. These events are not referred to in the Battalion War Diary or George's diary but all the men of the battalion must have been aware of what was happening and each must have had their own views on the level of culpability of their comrades in arms.

On 30 June the troops received a message from the Corps Commander, Lieutenant General Sir A.G. Hunter-Weston, known to the men as 'Hunter-Bunter', exhorting the officers and men to, '*stick it out, push on each to his objective and you will win a glorious victory and make your name in history*'. The fifty-one-year-old Scottish Laird was not well liked. His Staff Intelligence Officer was convinced he was mad, describing an occasion when:

He sent an officer home on duty to fetch his Xmas turkeys – then we prate on about economy and homilies are read to the men about waste. Futile little man. It is to my mind quite criminal that men like our ass from here should be given commands. Why should good men's lives be sacrificed unnecessarily by putting them under incapable leaders?

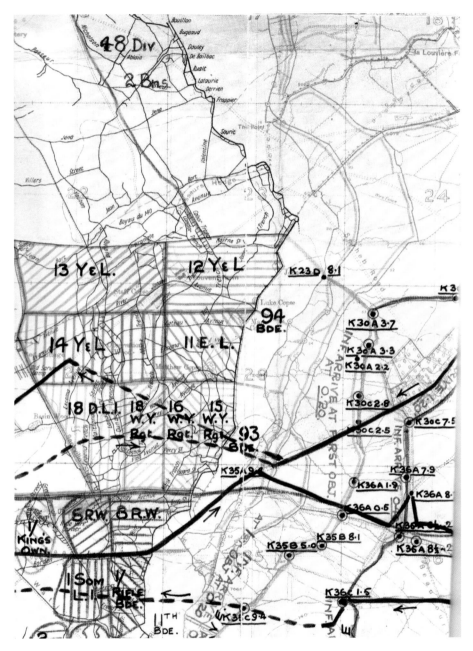

VIII Corps' plan of attack for 1 July 1916. The VIII Corps' plan shows the dispositions of 31st Division units and their attack objectives. The Corps' Commander, Lieutenant General Sir Aylmer Hunter-Weston, was seen as incompetent by his own staff officers.

In the early evening the men marched out of Bus and passed through the village of Colincamps on their journey to the front. In George's words: *'the boys went up to the trenches at 8.15 pm and after a good feed were in splendid spirits'*. The route from Colincamps to the front line in the early hours of the morning proved difficult due to congestion in the communication trenches and enemy artillery fire which caused a number of casualties, including the wounding of the Commanding Officer of 'D' Company, Captain Duckitt. It was not until 4.30 am on 1 July that the two battalions of the Bradford Pals were finally in position in their assembly trenches.

The path from Colincamps. 'Boys went up to the trenches at 8.15 pm and after a good feed were in splendid spirits.' The route to the trenches on the night of 30 June 1916 took the Pals through the village of Colincamps, where the villagers lined the street to watch them march past. From there the country path led directly to the mouth of the communication trench at the Sucrerie.

8

THE ATTACK ON THE SOMME

I have a rendezvous with Death
At some disputed barricade

ALAN SEEGAR, AN AMERICAN SOLDIER OF THE FRENCH FOREIGN LEGION,

WAS KILLED ON THE SOMME, 4 JULY 1916

The fateful day, Saturday 1 July 1916, dawned sunny and warm with mist in the hollows. It was said that larks could be heard singing.

General Rawlinson's instructions, set out in Operational Order No. 3, dated 1 July 1916, were simply stated:

1. *The Fourth Army will continue the attack.*

2. *A large part of the German Reserves have now been drawn in and it is essential to keep up the pressure and wear out the defence. It is also necessary to secure, as early as possible, all important tactical points still in possession of the Germans in their front line system and intermediate line, with a view to an ultimate attack on the German second line.*

Rawlinson, confident in the power of his artillery, was convinced there would be little resistance from the enemy and, conscious of the inexperience of the New Army battalions, urged a slow methodical advance but left the detailed planning to his subordinates. Lieutenant General Sir A.G. Hunter-Weston, the VIII Corps Commander, followed Rawlinson's advice and nineteen of his twenty-two battalions attacked in close formation, two or three paces between each man, line abreast, company by company. The Second Bradford Pals War Diary refers to the men '*advancing as if on parade*'. Not only were the elements of surprise and speed lost by the use of this inflexible and outdated tactic but the men's heavy loads meant that they were not capable of moving at much more than walking pace and perfect targets were offered to the enemy. Elsewhere along the fourteen-mile front, a handful of battalion commanders chose to attack in open formation using speed and cover but this did little to affect the overall outcome of the battle.

At 7.30 am, to the sound of their officers' whistles, the Leeds Pals and First Bradford Pals climbed out of their trenches to start the attack, followed at 8.40 am, as planned, by men of the Second Bradford Pals. What followed was a disaster. As forewarned by the abortive raid the previous night, the British artillery had not inflicted sufficient damage on the German fortifications. The field guns and medium calibre howitzers had failed to cut sufficient gaps in the wire or cause serious damage to the enemy's fortifications, not helped by as many as a third of the British shells being defective and failing to explode. As soon as the British barrage lifted, the German troops rushed out of their deep dugouts and manned the trenches and machine gun posts, firing red flares to summon help from the German artillery. The inexplicable blowing at 7.20 am of the nearby Hawthorn Ridge mine had given the enemy early warning that the long-awaited attack was about to start.

Opposite Serre, the Pals, encumbered with on average 70lbs weight of ammunition, grenades, iron rations, water bottles, entrenching tools and other equipment, walked into a hailstorm of rifle and machine-gun fire, and intense, accurate shelling. Machine-gun fire came from all directions, particularly crossfire from the German redoubt to the south known as the Quadrilateral or Heidenkopf Redoubt. Artillery fire was directed on the assembly trenches and came from hidden guns in the Gommecourt and Puiseux sectors. The Germans on the higher ground around Serre had an unobstructed view of the Pals as they came out of their trenches into the open. More than 2,000 troops of 93rd Brigade were densely packed into a constricted space not more than 500 or 600 yards in length and depth. They offered a rich choice of targets to the German gunners.

The Leeds Pals of the 15 West Yorkshire Regiment led the first phase of the attack. The Battalion War Diary account is short and terse due to all the battalion's officers being killed or wounded:

The attack was launched in successive waves. Each wave was met by a very sweeping MG fire. There had been an intense hurricane trench mortar bombardment but when the advance was made the enemy front line was thick with men. Fighting was hard and shelling heavy. Machine Gun fire was intense. Our casualties were 24 officers and 507 other ranks.

Private Hollins of 'D' Company of the Leeds Pals described the experience:

Not a man hesitated: in broad daylight last Saturday morning our lads got the order to advance. No sooner than the first lot had got over the parapet than the Germans opened up a terrific bombardment, big shells and shrapnel and their parapet was packed with Germans exposing themselves waist-high above the top and they opened rapid fire. They had machine guns every few yards and it seemed impossible for a square inch of space to be free from flying metal.

Close on their heels came the First Bradford Pals. The day's account from the War Diary of the First Pals starts:

Just before the infantry assault the medium Light Trench Mortars joined us but they did not prevent enemy Machine Gun fire opening at 7.30 am. The infantry assault commenced but owing to the large casualties including the loss of all officers no detailed narrative is possible.

The statement of Sergeant Major George Cussins, DCM gives a graphic account of what befell the First Pals:

Five minutes before 7.25 the enemy Machine Gun, Rifle Fire and Shrapnel were directed against the parapet of our assembly trench – the southern half of Bradford Trench – causing us to suffer considerably. A lot of men never got off the ladder but fell back and many fell back from the parapet in getting over. On getting out of the trenches to take up our position in front, we lost heavily through the line of shrapnel, machine gun and rapid rifle fire; by the time we attained our position in front of Bradford Trench, most of the officers, NCOs and many men were knocked out. At zero we advanced and continued to advance until the Company Headquarters, with which I was, found ourselves in front of the Battalion – all in front having been hit. We found ourselves then halfway between

'Leeds' and the front line. At this point I continued the advance – Captain Smith having been knocked out – and I carried on until we got to the front line. In our advance we passed the majority of 'A' Co halfway between 'Leeds' Trench and the front line, lying on the ground, killed or wounded. I found in the front line a good many of the 15th West Yorks, what was left of the DLI company attached to us, also a few of the KOYLI. I found no officers or NCOs of any of the above regiments, or my own regiment. The order came to 'bear off to the left' – I proceeded to do this and found Lt Jowett of my Regiment, who ordered me to try to collect and organise the few men who were left with a view to advancing again. At this moment the enemy started shelling our front line very heavily with Shrapnel and High Explosive – this would be nearly one hour after zero but of course I cannot give the correct time. Within a very short time all the men we had collected were knocked out – including Mr Jowett who gave me instructions to make my way back to Brigade Headquarters and report that there were no men left. He told me that he had already sent back to Battalion Headquarters 3 or 4 times but without success. This would all be about one hour to an hour and a half after zero and I could make out that some of our men were then advancing towards the enemy lines and must have been quite close up to the German parapet as I saw some of the Germans show themselves over the parapet, shoot at, and then throw bombs at what must have been some of our men.

Two days later, Second Lieutenant Laxton, the First Bradford Pals Intelligence Officer, who was wounded in the attack, was sufficiently recovered to be able to give an account of what had happened on the morning of 1 July:

At 5 minutes to zero, Major Guyon (First Pals Commanding Officer), Ransome and myself left our headquarters for the front line. We had only been by Sap A about two minutes when Major Guyon was struck through the helmet by a bullet. Ransome and I were alongside at the time and bandaged him up, though unconscious and apparently dying, the wound being in the temple. We were obliged to leave as things did not appear to be going well. We urged the men on and saw the columns advancing over Leeds Trench, one being led by Captain Pringle. Things seemed to stop, men were falling and no-one advancing over our front line. Stead was in the front line with a few men, which we scraped together for a rush. Stead and I scrambled out and the men tried to follow but were mown down by machine gun fire. I got about 15 yards before being hit by a bullet

Serre Number 3 Military Cemetery. The cemetery, situated in no man's land, with Serre village on the horizon, contains eighty graves of 93rd and 94th Brigade soldiers who were killed on 1 July 1916. The cemetery was created in 1917 after the German withdrawal to the Hindenburg Line and is typical of a small battlefield cemetery.

in the left knee and a piece of shrapnel in the right thigh and managed to crawl to a shell hole about five yards in front where I found Stead shot dead.

Twenty minutes before the Second Bradford Pals were due to attack, their Commanding Officer, Lieutenant Colonel Kennard, was ordered by Brigade Headquarters to investigate why the First Bradford Pals had been held up. The Battalion War Diary states:

8.20 am – message received from Brigade to the effect that the 16 West Yorks were held up and ordering the CO to go to Sap A to investigate. Lt Col Kennard accordingly went forward but was killed about 8.30 am by artillery.

8.40 am – Battalion left assembly trenches. Under heavy machine gun fire from time of leaving dead ground up to our front line trenches and an intense barrage of shrapnel and HE (high explosive). Casualties very heavy. Brigade advance was held up in front of German wire but 15th, 16th, 18th W. Yorks and one company of 18th DLI advanced as if on parade.

Lieutenant Colonel Kennard was replaced by his Second-in-Command, Major Carter. Although the Second Pals' casualties were just as severe as its sister battalions, sufficient officers survived the opening of the attack to submit reports of what happened to the men as they went forward. Their personal reports are contained in the Battalion War Diary along with Major Carter's overall summary of the battalion's actions. Captain Stephenson, who commanded 'C' Company (George's company), reported:

Most of the machine gun fire came from the direction of the Quadrilateral enfilading our advancing lines from the South after they had left our front line. No enemy seen in large numbers but they were seen on the enemy front line parapet. These must have had good cover in their front line during our bombardment either in dugouts or tunnels. The enemy artillery was a great surprise to our troops who had expected to find most of the enemy guns out of action. The enemy troops, standing on the parapet firing at our advancing troops, seemed to consider themselves quite safe from our guns. Could not our advancing troops not have laid down while our guns shelled the enemy down with shrapnel?

Second Lieutenant Cross of 'A' Company:

During the advance of the first platoon of the leading regiment a rapid rifle fire was opened on them directly they got out of the dead ground … and this was followed by heavy machine gun fire from direction of front line trenches south of Serre…. By the time I took my platoon out an intense bombardment was in progress on our front line and support trenches, canister bombers and heavy HE, also shrapnel, catching all the men as they reached the support line. This curtain of fire extended to our assembly trenches…. Our artillery seemed to me to have been concentrated mainly on German trenches, with good effect in smashing up trenches, but evidently did not smash up their dugouts, judging by the rifle fire.

Lieutenant Howarth, Officer Commanding 'B' Company:

The position of the enemy's machine guns appeared to be from the south and was cross fire. Most of the artillery came from Puiseux and was a remarkable curtain of fire. It seemed to me that the artillery played too long on the enemy's front line instead of putting out the Hun's guns owing to the wonderful dugouts used by the Huns.

The immediate objective of the new Commanding Officer, Major Carter, was to gather together the survivors who were widely scattered among the forward trenches and then construct a defensive line to ward off any German counter attacks. Major Carter's account of the first hours of the action contained in the Battalion War Diary illustrates the chaotic conditions which faced the survivors:

Owing to the unexpected resistance of the enemy the Brigade was compelled to retire and a verbal message to this effect was received. For a time the first and second line was vacated and the Battalion was broken up in retiring through our trenches. The majority of our casualties occurred between Leeds Trench and our own wire and were due chiefly to machine gun fire from flank and front. Three very heavy barrages were formed along our line which hampered the advance and caused other casualties before reaching Leeds trench. A number of other casualties were caused by indirect frontal machine gun fire. Approximate casualties; 16 officers, 400 other ranks.

Major Carter was clearly concerned that there might be criticism from senior officers that the battalion had retreated and not advanced as had been ordered. In the Battalion War Diary he goes to great pains to describe how during the day and through the following night he had made repeated and often unsuccessful attempts to contact Brigade Headquarters by telephone and by sending runners, and also how he had worked to construct defensive positions to block any enemy counter-attack.

With a scratch force of six officers and 120 men, Carter successfully held a defensive line in Monk Trench, just behind the empty front line. The Pals continued to hold their defensive positions for another three days with reinforcements from the 18th Battalion Durham Light Infantry and the pioneers of 12 KOYLI, the miners' battalion. In his memoirs, Captain Ede England of the miners' battalion describes the work asked of his men:

12 Battalion KOYLI as the only unit in the front line approaching anything like completeness, found itself installed as the defender of that portion of the British front. Our men lay on the parapet along a wide trench of unsavoury memory known as Sackville Street…. On 2 July, the Battalion acting as divisional reserve withdrew to the rear trenches and occupied itself day and night with the reconstruction of our battered defences, the location and salvation of the wounded who lay about the field in scores and the burial of the dead…. In the late afternoon of 4 July, the Battalion left the trenches and marched a sadder and wiser unit to the old camp in Bus wood. Approximate casualty list 197 all ranks.

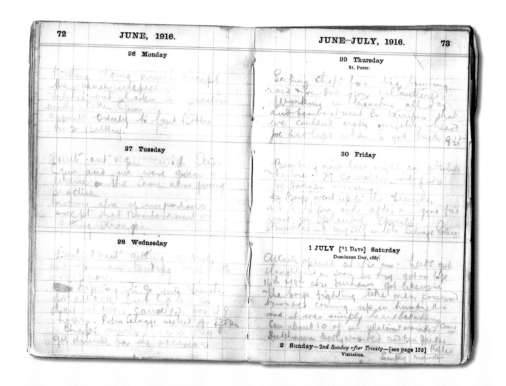

Diary entries for 26 June – 1 July 1916. 'Wounded coming up in hundreds and it was simply heartbreaking.' The two diary pages covering the entries for 26 June – 1 July 1916 show George's excellent handwriting and describe the events leading to the attack on 1 July 1916.

Throughout 1 July and the following few days, the 93rd Brigade wounded were brought to the Casualty Clearing Stations in the rear areas. George witnessed the sad procession:

1 July 1916 – Wounded coming up in hundreds and it was simply heartbreaking. Saw about ten of our platoon's wounded come in. Hutchinson badly wounded and Ben Parker killed. Simply murder.

2 July 1916 – Our lads back in their own line and almost 500 of the whole Brigade left. Attack a failure and according to one of the 4th Division it was wonderful how the lads stuck it. Artillery fire simply mowed them down. Much worse than anything seen before.

3 July 1916 – Still at Bus on salvage – very busy. Went down to the trenches with limber at night. Very exciting indeed and had a lucky escape – shrapnel bursting overhead.

4 July 1916 – Went down to railhead at night and called into Louvencourt coming back. Boys coming into Louvencourt from the trenches. Absolutely jiggered and sad over their awful losses.

Privates Hutchinson and Parker were from Batley. Hutchinson died of his wounds on 27 July. The body of the eighteen-year-old Ben Parker, a Leeds Pal and neighbour of George's in Staincliffe, Batley, was not found and he is commemorated on the Thiepval Memorial. Equal numbers of dead and wounded lay in no-man's land, often for several days and notable among them was Second Lieutenant Major William Booth of the Leeds Pals. Booth was a Yorkshire and England cricketer and as he lay dying in a shell hole, he was comforted by his wounded team-mate, Abe Waddington, a Bradford Pal. Waddington survived the war and continued his career with Yorkshire and England.

Conditions in the Advanced Dressing Station at Basin Wood near La Signy Farm, just behind the support trenches, were terrible. Doctors Roche and McTavish, the Bradford Pals' Medical Officers, worked tirelessly to save lives but many were beyond help. Corporal Albert Wood of the First Bradford Pals saw '*the most horrible sight*' of Dr Roche working at a trestle table with bodies '*piled like sandbags all around him*'. The two doctors later led stretcher parties into no-man's land to recover the wounded and were both awarded the Military Cross for their bravery. The few words in Dr McTavish's letter

Euston Road Military Cemetery. 'Our lads back in their own line and about 500 of the whole Brigade left.' Mass graves were dug at Euston Road Dump to cater for casualties who were brought to the nearby Advanced Dressing Station at Basin Wood. More than thirty Bradford Pals are buried at the Euston Road Military Cemetery.

to his friend in England capture the mood of the men and the conditions: *'You don't want to hear much about what I've seen lately. Still we have to lose some to lick the beggars. I'll never forget July 1st '16 as long as I live – it was an awful day.'* The citation for his Military Cross read:

> *For conspicuous gallantry and devotion to duty. Throughout severe fighting he was responsible by his energy, courage and contempt for danger in saving a large number of severely wounded who would have been left in the battered front line or in no man's land.*

The only significant success that day was on the far right flank of the attack where the

Liverpool and Manchester Pals battalions of 30th Division broke though and captured the village of Montauban. The French also captured the German first line of defence and this joint achievement, at relatively low cost, owed much to the plentiful supply of heavy calibre French artillery which was able to penetrate the deep German dugouts. 30th Division also made full use of thirteen 'Russian' saps which helped the British troops capture the enemy front line trenches before the Germans could leave their dugouts. Although General Haig was keen to exploit the breakthrough, Rawlinson, his more cautious subordinate, known for his 'bite and hold' tactics, chose not to send forward his reserve divisions or cavalry and the immediate opportunity was lost. Haig and Rawlinson came to the inescapable conclusion that the left flank attacks in the northern part of the battlefield area had failed totally and planned follow-up attacks were unlikely to succeed in the face of the formidable enemy fortifications. They turned their attention to attacking the southern flank but it took ten days to prepare and launch the attack on Mametz Wood, which saw desperate and bloody hand-to-hand fighting. After that, the offensive on the Somme became a four-month long battle of attrition.

Contemporary German accounts of the fighting at Serre refer to the unprecedented length and intensity of the British barrage, which was deadly to men keeping guard in the trenches but in many cases failed to destroy the deep bunkers. Otto Lais, of 8 Baden Infantry Regiment 169, described how once the British barrage lifted from the front line trenches to the second line objectives, the German soldiers raced to what was left of their defensive positions and opened fire with machine guns, rifles and mortars, followed by hand grenades where British troops came close to their wire:

For two hours and more, wave upon wave breaks against us. With incredible tenacity they run towards our trenches. In an exemplary show of courage and self-sacrifice, they climb from the safety of their jumping off position only to be felled, barely having reached our shot-up barbed wire. Those following behind take cover behind their dead, groaning and moaning comrades. Many hang, mortally wounded, whimpering in the remains of the barbed wire and upon the hidden iron stakes of the barbed wire barricade. The survivors occupy the slight slope around and behind the remains of the barbed wire and shoot at us like things possessed without much to aim at. They make cover for themselves from the bodies of their dead comrades and many of us fall in the fire. We shoot into the wire shreds, into the belt of barbed wire that winds to the earth. The hail of bullets breaks up at the wire and strikes downwards as an unpredictable crossfire into the protective slope. Soon the enemy fire dies out there as well.

His report describes the fate of the follow-up attacks and in particular how the British troops were caught by enfilade fire from machine guns in the Heidenkopf Redoubt as they left their second line trenches and moved into the open. The account tells of the rows of British dead and wounded in the 'misery' of no-man's land and how medical orderlies from both sides helped to remove the dead and wounded. This was an unpredictable business. In some parts of the battlefield there was an unofficial truce but in others rescuers were fired at and the recovery of the wounded had to be done under the cover of night. There were also British reports of some of the wounded being deliberately killed by German patrols.

Brigadier General Sir James E. Edmonds, the author of the Official History published in 1932, summarises the efforts of 31st Division with these words:

The extended lines started in excellent order but gradually melted away. There was no wavering or attempting to come back. The men fell in their ranks, mostly before the first 100 yards of No Man's Land had been crossed. The magnificent gallantry, discipline and determination displayed by all ranks of the North Country Division were of no avail against the concentrated fire of the enemy's unshaken infantry and artillery whose barrage has been described as so consistent and severe that the cones of the explosions gave the impression of a thick belt of poplar trees.

Thiepval Memorial. Designed by Sir Edwin Lutyens, the memorial contains the names of 74,000 men who were killed on the Somme and have no known grave.

9

THE COST

He fell: But yielded not his English soul –
That lives out there beneath the battle's roll.

SERGEANT JOHN WILLIAM STREETS, YORK AND LANCASTER REGIMENT, WHO DIED ON 1 JULY
1916 IN THE ATTACK ON SERRE VILLAGE. PUBLISHED 1917

The cost in lives of the battle far outweighed the meagre gains in ground taken. On
the first day, 57,000 British troops were killed, wounded, missing or taken prisoner
– approximately half of the men who were in the attack. Of these, more than 19,000
men were killed or died of their wounds and, altogether, this was the worst day in the
history of the British Army. Casualties on this scale were unprecedented and it took
some time before the generals gained an accurate appreciation of the losses. General
Haig, believing that the casualty figure was around 40,000, was of the view that they
'*cannot be considered severe in view of the numbers engaged and the length of front attacked*'.
He was also unfairly dismissive of the efforts of Lieutenant General Sir A.G. Hunter-
Weston's VIII Corps implying that they had been reluctant to leave their trenches.
Hunter-Weston himself displayed a measure of complacency if not self-deception in a
letter to his wife:

> *The men are not in the least bit down hearted at their losses, and are as fit and happy as*
> *can be, working away to clear the battlefield and getting ready for our next operations.*
> *I was of course disappointed that we did not get through but not worried or upset. I had*
> *done my little best and was well repaid by the courage and discipline of the troops. Next*
> *time we will succeed.*

The causes of the disaster are still a matter of controversy. Poor leadership certainly
played a major part with many of the senior staff displaying aspects of incompetence

all too common among the narrow class from which most of them came. As well as an arrogant underestimation of the enemy, there was a resistance to embrace new tactics. The latter failing can be seen in the way the infantry advanced as if on parade, as well as a slowness to adopt new technologies and weapons, evident in the lack of heavy artillery and the lack of flexibility in its deployment. There was an aversion to reconnaissance and intelligence, and last-minute raids and patrols were no substitute for thorough and meticulous analysis of the enemy's dispositions and intentions. The Great War generals were addicted to spirited frontal assaults which, against well-sited machine guns and concealed artillery batteries, had the inevitable effect of mass casualties, the extent of which could only leave the impression of a callous disregard for the lives of their men.

The generals were well aware that the new Kitchener battalions lacked experience and were insufficiently trained in tactics and manoeuvre, but they did not compensate for this inadequacy in either tactical planning or deployment. The Bradford Pals were on the Somme for three months before the battle but a reading of the Battalion War Diary and George's personal diary shows that much of this time was spent on labouring tasks and manning the front line, and less than a week on practising the attack. The Bradford Pals were not alone in this regard among the Kitchener battalions and it seems strange that the New Army was asked to make the largest contribution by far to the first day attack without stiffening from Regular Army battalions. Indeed, 31st Division had no experienced Regular Army infantry units in its establishment.

Lessons were learned from the debacle of the first day of the Somme and in the following phases of the battle the 'creeping barrage', where the infantry closely followed the belt of bursting shells, became a regular feature of major assaults. Improvements were made in heavy gun, ammunition supply and tactical training but successful use of these more effective measures required high levels of proficiency in the artillery units and well-trained infantry who had confidence in the artillery supporting them. These were skills which could not be learned overnight.

The casualties in 31st Division were so severe that the division was withdrawn from the line to be replaced by troops from 48th Division. In total, 31st Division suffered almost 4,000 casualties, including 150 officers. As we have seen, it took until 4 July to extricate the men from the trenches and the Second Bradford Pals War Diary describes the difficult conditions they faced:

Journey out of trenches occupied a long time and was rendered difficult by a very heavy storm of rain. Trenches in places four feet deep in water. Journey delayed by stretcher cases and to 94 Brigade by accident using Railway Avenue instead of Northern Avenue. Men dumped overcoats at Euston Dump as they came out and marched to Louvencourt.

93rd Brigade lost 1,600 men – slightly more than 94th Brigade – and approximately 40 per cent were killed. More than half the dead were less than twenty-two years of age. Both Bradford Pals battalions lost around 70 per cent of their attacking strength. In the Second Pals, more than 120 officers and men were killed and over 300 wounded or missing.

Some of the Bradford Pals are buried in Serre Number 3 Military Cemetery which contains eighty graves and is situated in no-man's land opposite Serre village.

More than thirty are buried at Euston Road Military Cemetery near the site of the Advanced Dressing Station at Basin Wood where the Battalion Medical Officers worked heroically. Some are to be found in the two large 'concentration' cemeteries, Serre Numbers 1 and 2 Military Cemeteries but many of the dead have no known grave and their names are among the 74,000 listed on the Thiepval Memorial a mile or two away.

The people of Bradford heard of the battle on the first day itself, the *Bradford Daily Telegraph* reproducing a wildly optimistic communiqué from Army Headquarters:

A message from the British Headquarters dated Saturday 9.30 says: At 7.30 am this morning vigorous attacks were launched by the British Army on a front of about 20 miles, north of the Somme. The assaults were preceded by a terrific bombardment, lasting one and a half hours. The British have already occupied the German front lines. Many prisoners have been taken and as far as can be ascertained our casualties have not been heavy.

Other early reports in the *Bradford Daily Telegraph* mirrored the army's optimistic communiqués and it was not until 6 July that the names of Bradford casualties started to appear in the national *Daily Telegraph*. The New Army Pals battalions were recruited from close-knit communities and over the next few days, as the casualty lists appeared in the local papers, the extent of the real losses became known with almost every family and every street being affected. On 10 July the first of weekly special editions of the *Bradford Weekly Telegraph* was published containing photographs of the dead and wounded and first-hand accounts of the battle, such as that from Private Chapman of the Second Pals:

> *I am indeed lucky to be alive after our terrible experience. I fear very many of both Bradford battalions are no more and the same applies to the Leeds battalion. I walked over our dead in scores both in the open and in the trenches when working my way back.... First July will never fade from my memory. I thank God that I am left to live, yet it is really miraculous.*

The army authorities were keenly aware of the need to sustain morale on the Home Front and urged the population to believe that the sacrifice was not in vain. On 18 July the *Yorkshire Post* published the following letter from Major Carter, the new Commanding Officer of the Second Bradford Pals, to Mr Howarth, the Mayor of Bradford:

> *I feel it is my sad duty to write to you on behalf of the officers, NCOs and men to express our sympathy with all those in Bradford who have suffered loss and sorrow as a result of the fighting on 1 July. We are a Bradford battalion and Bradford's grief is ours: more so as all those who fell were our comrades, men with whom we had all served, men we loved for their cheeriness and gallantry in the trenches, for their devotion to duty and their pride of battalion during all their period of soldiery. What these men did can be surpassed by none – it can only be equalled in death and self-sacrifice. Let therefore Bradford wives and children who are all stricken in sorrow raise their heads and with strength show the world that they are sad but not bent with sorrow; that they grieve but are not broken with grief; that they are – as their fathers, brothers and husbands were – willing to have made the sacrifice. We soldiers too are sad, but are prouder to have been their comrades. Bradford's is the highest glory; she should be prouder still. She bred them and gave them to her country.*

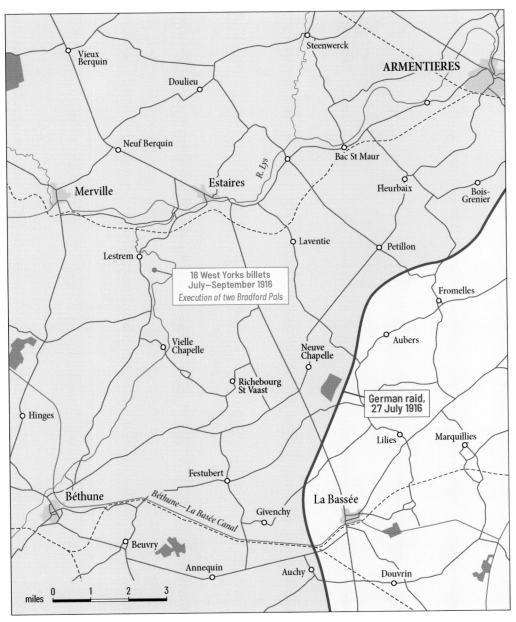

Neuve-Chapelle and Givenchy, July – October 1916

10

NEUVE-CHAPELLE SECTOR,
9 JULY – 15 SEPTEMBER 1916

The function of the Court Martial is to preserve security by preserving the armed forces in a state of discipline. Just that. If it can be done with justice, so much the better: but it must be done.

MANUAL OF MILITARY LAW, 1914

31st Division's destination lay 50 miles to the north, near Béthune, a sector which had seen heavy fighting in 1915 at the battles of Neuve-Chapelle, Festubert, Givenchy, Aubers Ridge and Loos but was now supposedly quieter and therefore better suited to the task of rebuilding the division. On leaving the Somme the men were paraded at Louvencourt and sent on their way with an address from the Corps Commander, Lieutenant General Sir A.G. Hunter-Weston, in which he '*congratulated all ranks on the discipline and determination shown during the attack and saluted the 31st Division as heroes of whom he was proud to be a comrade*'. (Battalion War Diary, 5 July 1916)

The Pals had a four-day, 30-mile march to the railhead at Conteville. George, who was still busily engaged at Bus on salvage duties, caught up with them by motor bus at Fienvillers on 7 July. On arrival, and in a rather laconic tone he notes, '*wanted for working in Orderly Room*'. The Orderly Room was a key part of a battalion's headquarters. Under the command of the Adjutant, it was situated alongside the Commanding Officer, acting as his personal staff and was responsible for the issuing of operational orders and the administration of the thousand men in the battalion. A Sergeant (the Orderly Room Clerk) ran the day-to-day business with the help of three or four more junior ranking soldiers. As a full Corporal, George would have acted as the Sergeant's deputy and one of his many new tasks was the writing up of the daily entry in the Battalion War Diary (Army Form C.2118) which was then signed by the

Battalion's Commanding Officer. The War Diary, as the name implies, dealt solely with operational matters and George's distinctive handwriting features on many of its pages.

When the battalion was in the front line, the Orderly Room staff usually accompanied the Commanding Officer and would occupy dugouts in the second or third line of trenches, which gave better protection from enemy artillery and small arms fire but by no means guaranteed safety. My father did not say why he was chosen for a new job in the battalion headquarters but his peacetime profession gave him the necessary skills and the contact he had had with Major Carter, the new Commanding Officer, may have been a factor. It is clear from his diary that he welcomed the change and the involvement it brought in the administration of the battalion's business.

On 10 July the Pals reached their new billets at L'Eclème, a small village about 7 miles northwest of the industrial town of Béthune, where they spent a week cleaning up, training and receiving reinforcements. Many of the new troops and future reinforcements were not from Bradford or West Yorkshire. The army authorities quickly realised that heavy losses of men from a specific locality had a disproportionate impact on morale in the men's hometowns and adopted a policy of mixing the composition of reinforcements to infantry battalions. The gradual reduction in the number of the volunteers, and the consequential introduction of conscription from January 1916, effectively ended the concept of Pals battalions.

From L'Eclème the Second Pals marched east to the small town of Lestrem, which was about 4 miles from the front line at Neuve-Chapelle. Although George described Lestrem as '*a splendid little place and you can get a jolly good feed cheap. Much nicer than the Somme District*', the nearby battlefield was a different matter. The area was part of the flat marshy plain of the river Lys, which stretches from Saint-Omer to Béthune. The battles of 1915 had destroyed the dykes and drainage system and, unlike the chalkland of the Somme, it was impossible to dig deep trenches. The front line was a series of breastworks formed largely of sandbags standing above the level of the ground. The breastworks were easily destroyed by shellfire and it was extremely difficult to move safely around the trenches, which were little more than shallow water-filled drainage ditches. Rotting bodies from the 1915 battles lay unburied in no-man's land. In his memoir, Captain Ede England of the KOYLI Pioneers Battalion describes the difficulty of constructing sound defences:

31st Division troops in Béthune sector, 1916. 'Our dugout very dangerous at night. Germans seem to have a machine gun trained across the top.' After the Battle of the Somme the Pals were moved to the Béthune sector for rest and reinforcement. The photograph shows 31st Division troops in the typical trench conditions of the flat, marshy plain of the River Lys.

We were in what could be described as the Fen District of Northern France. The countryside was thickly covered with dykes, big and small, deep and shallow, and as the water level was only a few inches below the surface of the ground it was impossible to dig trenches as we knew them then. Instead of that, trenches, or rather breastworks, had to be built of tiers of sandbags about six feet high and consequently they were easily damaged…. It was highly embarrassing when sheltering behind an apparently solid wall of English sandbags to observe a German bullet arrive with a slap on the rear wall of the trench … the walls were only one sandbag thick instead of four and bullets passed through as easily as butter.

For their part, the Germans had the advantage of holding the higher ground on Aubers Ridge and had built an extensive network of concrete dugouts and pillboxes, often supplied with electricity piped from the nearby city of Lille, a luxury generally not available to the British troops.

On 13 July the Corps Commander addressed all the officers of 93rd Brigade with the aim of '*inspiring an offensive spirit in connection with raids*' (Battalion War Diary) and further encouragement was given on 20 July by the Acting First Army Commander, General Richard Haking, who inspected the troops and '*congratulated them on their smart appearance and remarked that he had no doubt whatever of their being just as steady under fire as they were on parade*'. (Battalion War Diary) That very day, Haking, a protégé of Haig, had overseen the disastrous attack by the British 61st division and Australian 5th Division at nearby Fromelles, which cost 7,000 casualties with no gain. Although he had been instructed by Haig to make the attack in the hope that German reserves would be diverted from the Somme battlefield, Haking's conduct of the Fromelles action was inept. He faced severe criticism, not least from the Australians, and, despite Haig's support, he was passed over for further promotion.

Immediately on entering the trenches at Neuve-Chapelle on 27 July, the Second Pals were met by a surprise German raid which wiped out most of 'B' Company. Eighty men were killed, wounded or taken prisoner. At around 9.30 pm the Germans directed an intense artillery bombardment on the two battalions holding the line either side of 'B' Company's position. Having successfully isolated 'B' Company, some thirty Germans dressed in black infiltrated their trenches and killed or took prisoner most of the troops they found. The Battalion War Diary gives a minute-by-minute account of how the attack developed, the steps taken to establish contact with 'B' Company and attempts to launch a counter-attack. Chaos and confusion reigned and although the raid, which started at 10.00 pm, only lasted half an hour, it took until 7.00 am the following morning to secure the front line with reinforcements and re-establish order.

After the attack, Lieutenant Colonel Carter, the Commanding Officer, spoke to witnesses and drew up a summary of what happened:

Appendix 'C' to War Diary – further information of German raid

The enemy entered our front line in two parties; one near Bay 80 and the other near Bay 100. The strength of each party was about 16, and the whole were in charge of an officer. On entering the trench these two parties worked inwards and on uniting left our line with several prisoners. Their arrival was very unexpected and rapid. It seems that they made use of the old trench from the SEVEN SISTERS to point S5.c 40, and then parallel to our front line opposite S 11.1. They advanced under cover of the smoke from their bombardment and immediately after the lift.

Many of our men were surprised in their dugouts which were lit up with the aid of electrical torches carried by the enemy. The enemy were armed with revolvers and bombs. Our witness states that several of the enemy inflicted slight wounds on prisoners, presumably with the idea of preventing escape. It is noteworthy that that one of our men was bandaged up by a German who had wounded him with a bomb and then a revolver.

Those of our men who were not taken prisoners, did not throw bombs at the enemy, fearing that they would hurt their own men. Some of them, however, made use of their rifles.

L/Cpl Denton was taken prisoner in the trench and taken about 300 yards towards the German line. He there knocked over his man and escaped, reaching our lines about 10am. He was slightly wounded. He reports that Lt Howarth, Lt Watson and 2nd/Lt. Walton were all made prisoners. The enemy had two parties each of about 16 or 17 men, with one officer. They cleared the trenches and joining forces left our line with the prisoners. He thinks the enemy stayed in our line for 20 minutes or half an hour.

Another man, who was left behind owing to his wounds, judges that they remained a quarter of an hour.

It is reported that the enemy took away a box or two of machine gun ammunition (belts) and a Vickers Gun.

It has been reported that during the above operations our own Artillery was firing very short, most of the shells bursting in or on our side of our wire.

A dead German was searched; the only thing that gave any information, however, was his pass for leave from 1 April 1916. He belongs to the 3rd Ersatz Company of the 245th Ersatz Battalion, Reserve Infantry Division. A belt was found in our trenches, belonging to a German reported to be wounded. This man apparently belongs to the 121st Regiment.

One of the captured men was Sergeant Dickie Bond, a Bradford City and England footballer, which, given his fame, must have been very pleasing to the Germans. Bond played eight times for England and more than 300 times for Bradford City. Bond, noted for his profanity, missed the 1911 FA Cup Final against Newcastle, which Bradford City won 1-0, as he was serving a suspension for the use of offensive language directed at Arsenal supporters in an earlier match. No doubt he cursed long and hard at being captured but good fortune was on his side. He survived captivity and after the war was able to resume his football career.

George's diary entries for 27, 28 and 29 July give a detailed account of the number and type of casualties of the raid, an indication that his role in the Orderly Room gave him access to accurate information of the battalion's business:

27 July 1916 – Set off for the line at 10 am and arrived at HQ at 3pm. Decent dugout so nothing to grouse at. 10.30 pm Germans smashed our trenches in and raided 'B' Company's sector. Hellish bombardment and the casualties were very heavy. Germans took some prisoners back.

28 July 1916 – Trenches smashed in with last night's affair and our losses heavy – three officers prisoners and two killed (Humphreys and Cross), six men killed, thirty-seven wounded and thirty taken prisoner. 'B' Company twenty-three men left – Dickie Bond prisoner. German trophies brought in – helmet, entrenching tool, twenty bombs and a lot of personal property etc. Saw some German bread tickets. Ten wounded today.

29 July 1916 – Nothing much doing in the line but repair work. Another of 'A' Company wounded in the afternoon. Talking to Lance Corporal Denton who was taken prisoner but escaped the following morning. German machine guns very busy tonight and heavy bombardment on the left.

The enemy raid prompted extensive patrolling of no-man's land in an attempt to gain intelligence and forestall similar raids. The Battalion War Diary describes the work of three patrols, provided by the Leeds Pals, each of three or four men, on the night of 29 July:

First Patrol – Went out from Vine Street at 11 pm returning at 12.30 am. Got to within 30 yards of the German wire and the enemy was seen working on it in small parties and also grass cutting. The grass was cut for two or three yards in front of his wire.

Second Patrol – Went out at 10.15 pm and reached a point about 30 yards from the enemy's wire. The grass was at least 2 feet high and reached to the wire; this and the presence of working parties all along the parapet prevented a close examination. Work was proceeding on the wire on both sides. A Very light was sent up on its right seemingly from a covering party in front of the wire. Patrol returned at 1am.

Third Patrol – Went out at 11 pm. They got within 20 yards of the enemy wire and went along it for about 100 yards. No work was going on but talking could be heard in the trench. The patrol got lost owing to the mist. They crossed two ditches parallel to our line about 1 foot deep in water and mud and also old trench running towards German lines. The patrol think they were heard as lights were sent up and a M.G. turned on them. They returned at 4.30 am.

Bradford Pals at leisure. 'Went to Merville again with Willie. Had our photographs taken together and also had a decent time.' This photograph, taken on 25 July 1916, shows George, third from left, with Willie Armitage, his future brother-in-law, fourth from left.

Rest periods allowed the men to visit the nearby towns of Lestrem and Merville. For George, '*Madame's across the road*' at Lestrem was a popular venue, as evidenced by the celebration of Lance Corporal Cyril Burgoyne's 21st birthday on 6 August – '*Duck, beans and potatoes, wine etc. Oh! What a spread. Cyril got tipsy.*' Lance Corporal Cyril Burgoyne was one of George's new Orderly Room colleagues and a close bond was formed between the clerks. On a visit to Merville, George and Willie Armitage, his future brother-in-law, had their photographs taken by an enterprising French photographer. On collecting the prints ten days later, George returned to his billets with '*Australian Engineers who were extremely noisy – drunk*'. Throughout his diary, references to French towns and villages and their residents are invariably favourable – a view not shared by some less than charitable soldiers who found the prices in the estaminets to be extortionate and the welcome not always friendly.

Although it was regarded as a quiet sector, there was a steady drain of casualties from the ever-present artillery, snipers and trench mortars. During the month of August the battalion spent more than twenty days in the front line or in reserve in the Neuve-Chapelle and Festubert sectors and the following extracts from George's diary reveal the routine and associated stress that this entailed:

1 August 1916 – Still in the trenches and having a much better time than I had expected. Fritz sending his Minenwerfers over all day. Weather absolutely splendid.

2 August 1916 – Nothing much doing in morning but afternoon heavy shelling on our front line. A few casualties in 'A' Company and the 16th. Joe Jubb killed from Batley.

3 August 1916 – Same old carry on and with the exception of his Minnies Fritz did not bother us very much. Our guns pretty active all day.

The Minenwerfer was a trench mortar, the most common of which was a 76mm weapon firing a 10lb bomb. The sound of its passage through the air caused the troops to christen it a 'Minnie'. Private Joe Jubb, aged twenty-nine, was a Leeds Pal and the son of a prominent Batley mill owner. He was a pupil of Batley Grammar School and trained as an architect. Joe was shot by a sniper whilst on wiring duties and is buried in the St Vaast Post Military Cemetery at Richebourg-L'Avoué.

On 10 August the Bradford Pals went into the trenches in the Festubert Sector for an unusually lengthy spell of ten days in the front line. They endured intermittent shelling, sniping and machine-gun fire, which according to the Battalion War Diary inflicted little more than a dozen casualties, one of which was accidental and another a self-inflicted wound. The War Diary describes typical artillery exchanges on 17 August:

> About twenty to thirty 77mm (HE and shrapnel) were fired at our front line in retaliation to our Stokes guns. About 5.40 to 6 pm about thirty 77mm, with a few 4.2 (shrapnel and HE) were fired. Our own artillery fired on enemy front line at intervals between 9 am and 12 noon. Casualties nil.

George's account of this period adds some colour to the rather terse War Diary entries:

> 12 August 1916 – I was looking at La Bassée through some glasses. Fine sight – chimney stack, water tower and pit head stands out prominently. Got sniped at so promptly ceased observing. Saw the crater at Givenchy. Night was exceptionally quiet.

> 13 August 1916 – Heavy bombardment on the left though it sounds miles away. Our part of the line seems very quiet just now. Having occasional casualties but nothing very bad.

> 14 August 1916 – Still very quiet except for the usual trench mortar and MG activity. Dugout very dangerous at night. Germans seem to have a machine gun trained across the top.

> 16 August 1916 – Quiet up to 8.30 pm when the Germans got vexed with a battery just behind us and starting sending 5.9s over. Expected every minute our dugout would be blown in but good fortune stuck to us and we missed it. Lasted about an hour. Quiet night.

> 17 August 1916 – Bit of a bumping in the afternoon but nothing special. Started raining very heavy about 6 pm and went on till 7 pm. Trenches sloppy. Quiet night except for snipers and MGs who were very active indeed.

> 18 August 1916 – Harold Cullum killed early this morning. Our guns provoked Germans

into bombarding us about 4.30 am. Put over a hell of a lot of stuff (4.2s and 5.9s) into second line for thirty minutes. Relieved from front line by Leeds at 9.30 pm and went into reserve line.

19 August 1916 – Spent the day in bed resting but in evening went up to see 'C' Company who were billeted just behind. This place appears to me to be more dangerous than the firing line. Battery of Naval guns behind and our canvas hut simply lifts when they are fired.

The thirty-four-year-old Private Harold Cullum of the Second Bradford Pals came from Bradford and is buried at the Le Touret Military Cemetery. George was struck by the prominent features of the coal mines around La Bassée and Loos to the south. The ground either side of the Béthune–La Bassée canal was noted for another more lethal type of mine, and the area was pockmarked with one hundred mine craters. The reference to the crater at Givenchy is probably to the 'Red Dragon Crater', which was blown by the Germans on 22 June 1916. At that time it was the largest mine exploded on the Western Front with a crater more than 100 feet across and was named the 'Red Dragon Crater' in honour of the 2nd Battalion Royal Welsh Fusiliers who lost fifty-five men in evicting the Germans and holding the crater against counter-attacks. It lost its title as the largest mine nine days later when the British mines on the Somme at Lochnagar and Hawthorn Ridge were exploded on 1 July 1916.

Aviation played a key part in the artillery battle with the two-seater spotting aircraft of both sides providing target information to artillery batteries. In the early part of the Somme offensive the Royal Flying Corps fighter planes, or 'scouts' as they were known, had succeeded in protecting the slow and vulnerable two-seaters but the introduction of the Albatros D1 in August 1916 gave the Germans air supremacy. The Albatros was the first scout to be equipped with two machine guns firing through the propeller and not only was it better armed than the British aircraft but its powerful 160hp engine also gave it much greater speed. Baron von Richthofen, the 'Red Baron', made his first kill in September 1916 flying the Albatros which, for the next nine months, was to dominate the skies before the arrival of more advanced British planes, such as the Sopwith Camel, the Bristol Fighter and the SE5. German scout aircraft were not the only threat to the British artillery observation aircraft, which flew low and straight over the front lines seeking targets. George describes the demise of one of these planes:

22 August 1916 – In the evening one of our aeroplanes was hit directly with a German shell and came down in flames. The pilot and observer were both killed. A most horrible sight. A Taube came over and was attacked by four of ours but eventually it succeeded in escaping.

Following their lengthy spell in the front line trenches, the Pals spent a few days in reserve at Rue L'Epinette, a small village some 2 miles behind the front line, before returning to their billets at Lestrem on 2 September. Three days later, at 5.51 am on 5 September, Privates Wild and Crimmins, who had deserted their posts on the eve of battle on 30 June, were placed together against a barn wall at Lestrem and shot by a firing squad from their own battalion.

Even though the two men had been returned to front line duty on 27 July, where they had acquitted themselves well, they were still subject to court martial and this event duly took place on 21 August. The President of the Field General Courts Martial was Major Kennedy, the Commanding Officer of the First Bradford Pals supported by two other officers from 31st Division. The charge sheet for each man was identical and read:

When on active service deserting His Majesty's Service in that he, at Bus-lès-Artois on 30th day of June 1916 after being warned for duty as a ration carrier, absented himself from his Battalion until 1 pm on the 4th day of July 1916, when he gave himself up to the Military Police at Vignacourt.

The evidence presented was the same for each man and was not contested. Witnesses testified to the good conduct of both men and in the case of Private Wild evidence was given that he was suffering from shell shock caused by a number of near misses from artillery shells during the month of June 1916. While working at Euston Dump, he had been so badly affected that his officer, Second Lieutenant Thornton, had sent him back to camp. Private Oram, one of the witnesses, said:

I was in a working party with Private Wild near Euston Dump when heavy shelling commenced. I then noticed Private Wild was bad with shell shock so I reported him to the officer in charge. By shell shock I mean that he was all of a shake and ducked and quivered at every shell.

Private Crimmins apologised to the court for his actions:

I am very sorry for what I did. I had not the slightest intention of deserting. My father has been in the Army for twenty-seven years and I have five brothers now serving abroad. I have been in the trenches before and after this occurrence and tried to do my best.

The court decided that the men's actions had been deliberate and sentenced them both to death. In Crimmins's case, they recommended mercy on account of his good character and in Wild's case, mercy on account of, '*the nervous condition of the accused due to the explosion of a trench mortar projectile in the near vicinity of a sap in which he was working*'.

Not all the evidence was favourable and in attaching his comments to the court's findings, the Battalion Commander, Lieutenant Colonel Carter, expressed the view that both men were weak in character and that Crimmins had been led by Wild who he thought had deserted deliberately to avoid further active service. The staff at brigade, division, corps and army headquarters all concurred in the death sentences and on 1 September 1916 they were confirmed by Sir Douglas Haig and duly carried out four days later.

General Haig's motivation for imposing such a harsh and delayed sentence might be seen in the context of the continuing offensive on the Somme, which was not going well. There was a feeling among the generals that the New Army battalions, and 31st Division in particular, needed 'stiffening' and the failure to deal with the German trench raid on 27 July would not have gone unnoticed. The uncompromising attitude of the senior staff was amply demonstrated by Major General Wanless-O'Gowan, the 31st Division Commander, who is reported to have kicked away the flowers on the men's graves saying, '*these men are best forgotten*'.

Crimmins and Wild were buried near the place of execution but after the war were moved to the nearby Vieille-Chapelle New Military Cemetery where Private Wild's family, in contradiction to Major General Wanless-O'Gowan's words, placed the inscription '*Not forgotten by those who loved him most*' on the headstone of his grave.

The Battalion War Diary for the period 4 to 10 September is unusually sparse in detail, with just one short entry recording the provision of working parties for the front line. George's diary entry for 5 September says nothing more than, '*work and meals*'.

Some small degree of justice was done when, on 8 November 2006, Royal Assent was given to a pardon for all the 306 officers and men shot for desertion or cowardice in the Great War.

Following the execution, the Pals spent the next ten days at Lestrem and in reserve positions at Croix Barbee. Little of note occurred except for some German counter-battery fire which caused some alarm and which is recorded in George's diary entry for 14 September:

> *German aeroplane spotted a battery of guns 200 yards from us and their artillery sent about two hundred 6" shells over. Smashed the road to atoms but did not touch the guns. Two RFA wounded.*

Sergeant 'Jackie' Mallett, the Orderly Room Clerk and peacetime journalist, was sick during this period which caused George to be very busy but not sufficiently so that he could not find time to call in at Madame's in Lestrem for a '*good feed*' and for his Orderly Room colleague Cyril Burgoyne to return once again '*very joyful*' from a night out.

11

GIVENCHY SECTOR,
16 SEPTEMBER – 7 OCTOBER 1916

A 'crump' was a German 5.9 inch shell, its explosion when heard from a little distance, which was the most pleasant position from which to listen, sounded like a long drawn out c-r-r-ump.

A HISTORY OF THE 12TH (PIONEERS) KING'S OWN YORKSHIRE LIGHT INFANTRY, BY CAPTAIN R. EDE ENGLAND. FIRST PUBLISHED IN THE 1920S

On 16 September the Bradford Pals were relieved by the 4th and 6th Gloucesters and moved by motor lorry 10 miles south from Neuve-Chapelle to the Givenchy sector, which ran along the north side of the Béthune–La Bassée Canal. They were reinforced by a Cyclist Company from the IX Corps Reserve. Billets were provided in the grounds of Château la Gorre, which George found to be to his liking:

16 September 1916 – Taken from Croix Barbee to Gorre by Motor Lorry. Had a very nice journey. Got billets in the chateau. Magnificent building – very big indeed. Spent a good night. Had my clothes off once more.

Château la Gorre was a large house and estate on the outskirts of Béthune, about 3 miles to the west of the front line. The buildings were used as an officers' mess and headquarters, and accommodation for the many units in the area. The trench lines around Givenchy had a reputation for being dangerous which became immediately apparent the next day, causing George to write:

17 September 1917 – Up early and off to the line again. Entered the Givenchy Sector about 9 pm. Relieved 2nd Yorks. Extremely hot sector so there is likely to be plenty of fun.

Shell dropped about 20 yards off me – nothing touched me.

The Battalion War Diary describes the Pals' reception:

Quiet during the day. At 11.35 pm a 5 minutes bombardment of 'A' and 'B' front by 77mm HE a few light trench mortars and heavy machine gun fire as well as a number of rifle grenades in rapid succession. Remainder of the night quiet. Casualties nil.

The Givenchy sector and the area to the south of the canal, leading towards the mining town of Loos, had been extensively mined by both sides, with as many as one hundred mines being exploded during 1915 and 1916. The average width of no-man's land in this sector was 500 yards but it narrowed sharply in front of the village of Givenchy, which made mining an attractive proposition. The battalion did not experience any mine attacks during the three weeks it occupied the trenches at Givenchy but it suffered a number of casualties, with a number of the dead of 93rd Brigade being buried in the military cemetery in the grounds of Château la Gorre. The daily exchange of artillery, rifle grenade and trench mortar fire took its inevitable toll, as described in this entry in the Battalion War Diary:

27 September 1916 – Enemy sent a few 77mm HE in retaliation to our TMs about 11am and a battery of 5.9s fired at some point well behind our lines and near the canal about 7.30am. About 20 MTMs and a large number of aerial darts sent into centre company front. Over 100 rifle grenades sent over during morning on left company's sector, commencing in reply to our LTMs about 7am. Also, a large number on centre company front. Our own rifle grenades fired from centre company in retaliation. Casualties: 1 officer, 2/Lt R H Jones wounded (grenade), 2 OR killed and 8 wounded (grenade).

Captain Ede England of the Pioneer Battalion gave a colourful description of the types of shell fired at the Pals:

All shells were given slang names derived from their chief characteristics. A 'Black Maria' was a very heavy projectile that on explosion threw out a huge cloud of dense black smoke. 'Coal Box' and 'Jack Johnson' were other names given to German heavy shells. A 'crump' was the German 5.9 inch shell, its explosion when heard from a little distance, which was the most pleasant position from which to listen, sounded like a long drawn out c-r-r-ump. It was quite a common shell and much dreaded, as its penetrative power was considerable. A very distasteful missile was the 'whiz-bang'. Its name explains its nature. The most picturesque name of the lot was the 'woolly bear', a German shrapnel shell of large calibre that emitted at burst a big puff of brownish black smoke. 'Woolly bears' did great execution over our trenches on 1 July.

There was much relief when the Pals were withdrawn from the front line. George's diary entry for the final day of their spell in the trenches sums up the feeling:

29 September 1916 – Battalion relieved at 2.30 pm after having a rotten time. About 5 killed and 6 wounded. Jimmy Duggan and L/Cpl Stenhouse killed.

Duggan and James Thomas Stenhouse were both from the Second Bradford Pals and were among the original volunteers. The twenty-two-year-old Stenhouse from Bradford is buried at Gorre British and Indian Cemetery and Duggan at Choques Military Cemetery, 3 miles northwest of Béthune.

The town of Béthune, which in 1916 had a population of 15,000, was within easy walking distance of Gorre, and despite its proximity to the front line, at this stage of the war it was relatively undamaged. Most of the population had remained in the town, which offered a range of welcome facilities, such as shops, bars, estaminets and a number of places of lesser repute. George found it a *'splendid place more like home'* and when the Battalion was moved to billets at an orphanage on the outskirts of the city he was able to walk into the town at night and take tea. He clearly enjoyed exploring his surroundings and whilst at Gorre had enjoyed a *'nice walk down La Bassée canal'*, presumably in the direction of Béthune and not towards the front line at Givenchy. The German offensive in April 1918 brought the enemy to the outskirts of Béthune, when the town was almost totally destroyed by artillery fire.

The business of moving into and out of the trenches and from one part of the front to another required a great deal of administrative effort and the Battalion War Diary for this period contains a number of examples of the movement orders issued by the Orderly Room. Every detail had to be covered, including the arrangements for the

Commanding Officer's horse and groom. It was necessary to spell out which equipment had to be carried by the men and which could go on the horse-drawn General Service wagons or limbers. Occasionally, the luxury of light railways, motor lorries or buses was available. If the troops were moving within range of enemy artillery, care had to be taken to choose the safest route and to avoid large concentrations of troops in any one place. On leaving a position, the movement order would routinely state: '*company commanders will render a certificate that all billets have been left clean and tidy*'.

The Battalion did not stay long in the Givenchy sector and on 4 October it received orders to move south to the Somme where the battle still raged. This could hardly have been good news to the Pals but, after a short stay in Béthune, where a draft of fifty reinforcements was received, they enjoyed a couple of days' rest in their old billets at L'Eclème. George's account emphasises the importance of time out of the line:

5 October 1916 – Battalion moved from Béthune to L'Eclème near Busnes where we stopped when coming up to this part of the line –about 8 miles march. Tired. Got into the old billets.

6 October 1916 – Everyone in L'Eclème seemed pleased to have us back again. Not much work on. Walter went down to Lillers. Went up to 93rd Ambulance to see Lumb and Wilson.

7 October 1916 – Went down to Lillers at night with Sid Booth. Had a decent time and enjoyed the walk very much.

On 8 October the Pals entrained for Doullens and headed south, back to the Somme battlefield. Orders were received that day that the battalion was to come under the command of XIII Corps led by Lieutenant General Sir Walter Norris Congreve. The fifty-four-year-old Rifle Brigade officer had won the Victoria Cross in 1899 during the Boer War when he recovered captured guns while under fire. His son, Major Billy Congreve, an officer of The Rifle Brigade, was shot by a sniper on 20 July on the Somme. Billy Congreve was also a Victoria Cross holder, having won the medal for rescuing and tending wounded soldiers while under fire. He and his father were one of only three instances where both father and son won the Victoria Cross.

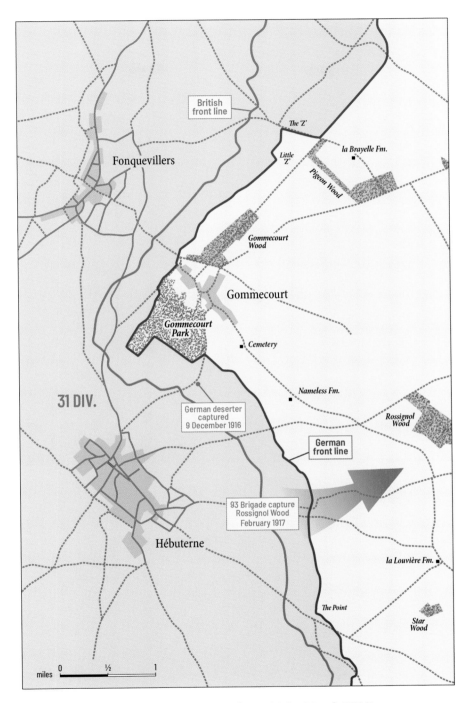

Hébuterne Sector, October 1916 – March 1917

Gommecourt Wood, 1916. 'Went with Mr Bowden to bring in a German deserter who was coming across no-man's land.' The Pals returned to the Somme in October 1916 and defended the village of Hébuterne opposite Gommecourt Wood, which is shown in the photograph taken by Royal Engineers surveyors from the British front line, some 500 yards distant from the wood. It was close to this spot, on 9 December 1916, that George assisted in the capture of a drunken German deserter.

12

THE SOMME: THE FINAL ACT, 8 OCTOBER – 19 NOVEMBER 1916

Gas! Gas! Quick, boys! – An ecstasy of fumbling,
Fitting the clumsy helmets just in time:
But someone still was yelling out and stumbling,
And flound'ring like a man in fire and lime …
Dim, through the misty panes and thick green light,
As under a green sea, I saw him drowning.

FROM 'DULCE ET DECORUM EST', BY SECOND LIEUTENANT WILFRED OWEN, MANCHESTER
REGIMENT. OWEN SERVED AT SERRE AND ST QUENTIN IN EARLY 1917 WHEN HE WAS
RETURNED TO THE UNITED KINGDOM SUFFERING FROM SHELL SHOCK

On 8 October the Bradford Pals returned to the Somme, occupying billets in a small village called Thièvres some 6 miles to the west of the front line village of Hébuterne which was located on the northern edge of the battle zone. The task of XIII Corps and 31st Division was to make one last attempt before winter set in to capture the village of Serre.

By October 1916, the offensive was in its fourth month and the modest gain of some 3 miles of German-held ground had cost more than 300,000 British casualties. General Haig knew that a major breakthrough was unlikely to be achieved but continued with the attack in the belief that the attrition of men and weapons would count more heavily against the German Army than the allies. Repeated 'bite and hold' attacks had indeed caused heavy German casualties, to the extent that Haig's Chief Intelligence Officer, Brigadier-General John Charteris, thought the enemy was near breaking point. Charteris, a protégé of Haig, had great influence among the General's inner circle. He was a brash, untidy officer, fond of a brandy and soda before breakfast and unpopular with the other staff officers. In particular, they thought he was over-optimistic in his assessments and exerted far too much influence on Haig's decisions. They referred to him as Haig's 'evil counsellor'.

British artillery preparation had improved since the early July assaults. More heavy guns were available and the concentration of large calibre artillery fire on key strong points was more successful in overwhelming the German defences. The development of the 'creeping barrage', which the infantry followed closely (often within 50 yards), helped to surprise German defenders sheltering in their dugouts but the improved British tactics still lacked the necessary precision and coordination between infantry and artillery to make a decisive breakthrough of the enemy lines. The task was made more difficult by German Army countermeasures, which included even deeper dugouts – improved trench layouts which allowed for rapid reinforcement and the use of shell holes away from trench lines in which machine gun teams were hidden which were very difficult to spot from the ground or in the air.

The battle also saw the first use of tanks when, on 15 September, thirty-two tanks went into action at Flers on the Albert to Bapaume Road. They proved to be mechanically unreliable and only nine managed to cross no-man's land, insufficient in number to gain much ground but enough to cause panic among the German infantry defending the front line trenches. The tank heralded a new type of warfare but it was not until the Battle of Cambrai in November 1917 that their potential was realised when a force of more than 400 tanks with strong infantry support and air cover broke through the German defences.

Just as the Bradford Pals were arriving on the Somme, Haig launched a major attack on 7 October along the Transloy Ridge in the centre of the front but the assault petered out on 20 October, again with only small gains. Torrential rain turned the already destroyed earth into a yellowish-grey mud which stuck to everything, jamming the mechanisms of guns and rifles and making movement by wheeled transport almost impossible. Men and horses sank into deep water-filled shell holes and often could not be rescued. In his memoir, *Twelve Days on the Somme*, infantry officer Sidney Rogerson describes the conditions he experienced in the closing months of the battle:

I had not gone twenty yards before I encountered the mud, mud which was unique even for the Somme. It was like walking through caramel. At every step the foot stuck fast, and was only wrenched out by a determined effort, bringing away with it several pounds of earth till legs ached in every muscle. No one could struggle through that mud for more than a few yards without rest. Terrible in its clinging consistency, it was an arbiter of destiny, the supreme enemy, paralysing and mocking English and German alike. Distances were measured not in yards but in mud. One of the war's great tragedies was that the High Command so seldom saw for themselves the state of the battle zone.

There had been no progress at all on the northern flank of the battle zone and Serre village remained firmly in German hands. The new billets of the Bradford Pals at Thièvres were outside the range of German shelling and the Pals spent two weeks receiving reinforcements, training and practising the attack. In the first half of October, almost 300 reinforcements were absorbed by the Second Pals, an indication of the extent of their losses in July and the amount of time needed to rebuild the battalion.

George's description of his new surroundings and his return to the Somme displays mixed feelings:

8 October 1916 – We arrived at Doullens about 8.30 pm and marched about 6 miles to Thièvres where we were billeted.

9 October 1916 – Still tired when I got up but had a good look round the village. It is rather cleaner than the average French village and the people are extremely nice for this district. (4 kilos from Bus our old place.)

10 October 1916 – Colonel Carter came back from leave about 2 am and roused the whole place – particularly me. Nothing particularly doing.

11 October 1916 – Battalion went out practising the attack. Reminded me of old times. Plenty German prisoners round here and they are a motley crowd.

14 October 1916 – Usual carry on. Walter Kellett gave us a fine selection of music on the village church organ. Played the old tune 'Somewhere' which sounded beautiful.

15 October 1916 – Church parade but could not get to it. Went to communion at night and enjoyed the service immensely.

16 October 1916 – Usual routine but expecting moving orders which came late at night.

17 October 1916 – Left Thièvres at 1 pm and marched to Warnimont Wood near Bus. Passed about 100 prisoners on the way. Went into Bus in the afternoon and the rotten hole had not altered a little although I hoped the Germans would blow it to bits.

18 October 1916 – Had a good look round this marshy like wood and it only made me more miserable than ever. Moving orders arrived very sudden and we went to Rossingnol Farm near Coigneux. Plenty prisoners here and they are a dusty looking crew.

George's dislike for Bus-lès-Artois and the nearby Warnimont Wood must have been prompted by the painful memories of 1 July and is clearly reflected in his low mood. His reference to the tune 'Somewhere' is to a popular hit song of the time. The lyrics were first published in 1901 and the song recorded in 1914. Its words convey thoughts of home which would have been deeply felt by young soldiers whose lives were in the balance:

> *Dusk and the shadows falling*
> *O'er Land and sea*
> *Somewhere a voice is calling*
> *Calling for me.*
>
> *Night and the stars are gleaming*
> *Tender and true.*
>
> *Dearest my heart is dreaming*
> *Dreaming of you.*

The new billets at Rossignol Farm were approximately 4 miles behind the front line and George thought it was strange that, although it was so close to the line, it had not been hit. The Pals occupied the sector of the line which ran through the village of Hébuterne, a mile north of their 1 July positions. John Masefield described Hébuterne and its neighbouring village, Gommecourt, which was held by the Germans:

Seen from our front line at Hébuterne, Gommecourt is a little more than a few red-brick buildings, standing in woodland on a rise of ground. A big spur of woodland known as Gommecourt Park thrusts out boldly from the village towards the plateau on which the British lines stood. This spur, strongly fortified by the enemy, made the greater part of the salient in the enemy line.

Charles Carrington (a Lieutenant in the Warwickshire Regiment) in his memoir *Soldier from the Wars Returning*, gave a similar description of the formidable German defences:

Gommecourt was an ideal tactical position, situated behind a reverse slope with observation posts forward on the crest, so that the defenders could not be directly observed. The strength of Gommecourt, heavily entrenched and wired against direct attack from the front, was in command of the country to either flank. The hundred guns ensconced in the 'dead ground' behind the wood could enfilade the whole British front to southwards and proved a decisive factor in the defeat of our 7th and 8th Corps on 1 July 1916.

The guns he mentions were those which caused such slaughter in the ranks of the Bradford Pals in July. On entering the front line on 21 October, the battalion was heavily shelled from the very same batteries situated behind Gommecourt Park. More than forty casualties were suffered in a six-day period, half of which were due to the effects of gas. The Battalion War Diary entries for 24 and 25 October show the difficult conditions facing the men:

24 October 1916 – Drafts came up to trenches from Rossignol Farm on night of 23 October and occupied support trenches on right of 'B' Company, supplying working parties. Casualties 2 OR wounded (artillery); 1 accidental (rifle).

25 October 1916 – Enemy rather more active than usual. From 11 pm – 11.15 pm enemy opened rapid fire on orchards E and SE of Battn HQ, obviously searching for one of our batteries. About 500 shells fired, including 4.2" HE, tear and gas shells. Gas shells caused several casualties. Our artillery very active all day. MTMs very active.
Patrol consisting of 2/Lt D A Gill, Sgt Quigley and Pte Sutcliffe left our lines at 8.45 pm to investigate German wire. Patrol proceeded east to German wire and about 100 yards

southwards where a clear gap about 30 feet wide was discovered and reconnoitred to within 10 yards of enemy parapet. Patrol was here observed by enemy sentry who fired 3 shots mortally wounding 2/Lt Gill. Machine gun also opened fire. Sgt Quigley and Pte Sutcliffe succeeded in bringing the officer's body back to our lines.

26 October 1916 – Battalion relieved by 18th Durham Light Infantry and went into billets in Sailly au Bois.

George's account of this period shows that his mood had not lifted at all:

22 October 1916 – Big bombardment started and our guns are making a hell of a row. Draft came in from Base – Young, Wood, Medley, Buckley and Naylor from Batley in it.

23 October 1916 – German shelling our batteries all day and night with gas tear shells so pleased I'm not up there. New draft went up to the line. Felt sorry for them.

24 October 1916 – Nothing particular occurred except the bombardment is still going on. Feeling anything but well but the MO's orderly is doing his best to keep me alright.

25 October 1916 – Boys having a beastly time in the line. Germans using gas and tear shells and a lot of our boys were gassed.

This appears to have been the first time the Pals had been exposed to gas attacks. The Germans had first used chlorine gas on the Western Front in a surprise attack at Ypres in April 1915, the gas being released from heavy cylinders placed in the front line. By 1916, both sides had developed artillery shells which could deliver a range of different gases accurately and quickly and which were not so dependent on weather or wind conditions. It seems that the Pals were attacked by a combination of toxic gas (phosgene mixed with chlorine) and tear gas, which was not toxic but caused great discomfort to the troops and impeded their military effectiveness.

George's weariness and lessening of enthusiasm is further reflected in his reaction to new billets at Coigneux:

30 October 1916 – Left Sailly 9 am and went to Coigneux. Billeted in huts in the muddiest place on God's earth – raining something awful all day. 10 men to a loaf of bread.

31 October 1916 – Usual carry on. Went scouting for grub. No bread issue and feeling awful peckish.

7 November 1916 – Left Coigneux and went into huts in the dell in Sailly – reserve for trenches. Pouring down all day so we were wet through and miserable.

8 November 1916 – Considerably drier this morning so not as miserable. Rain still the predominating feature of our life and I am heartily fed up with this war. Had a rotten letter from Lily.

Football and rugby games between the Orderly Room, Companies and Signallers brought temporary respite. George clearly enjoyed these games, despite some mixed results and having his '*wrist knocked up*' playing rugby. During his service in France he had been in and out of the front line for seven months and it was at least a year since he had had any leave. The threat of sudden death or injury was ever present and there was no end to the war in sight. It is hardly surprising that his morale should suffer and, in the final three months of the year, there are a number of references in his diary to attending church services and taking communion. Perhaps this brought him some solace or reassurance and a way of making sense of the dehumanising aspects of modern warfare.

The battalion moved back into the front line on 11 November, taking over the left sub-sector at Hébuterne. It must have been of some comfort when secure accommodation was to be had in the front line and George described the Battalion Headquarters in Vercingetorix Trench in Hébuterne as: '*a deep dugout used as battle HQ. Splendid place and very comfortable.*' This sentiment is echoed in Battalion Orders: '*Personnel of HQ, plus battalion bombers and observers will be in a large deep dugout 20 yards north of battalion headquarters.*'

The final phase of the Somme offensive opened on 12 November with, according to George: *Preparations being made for an attack. 'Terrific bombardment still going on. Very little retaliation from the "Bosche".'* The weather was bad, with snow on the ground and sheeting rain. Haig had been warned by his Corps Commanders and staff officers that the conditions on the battlefield and its approaches were the worst anyone had seen with movement and communication impossible. The ground was a stinking, rat-infested wilderness with thousands of unburied bodies and many unmarked graves. According to Charles Carrington:

The smell of burnt and poisoned mud – acrid is, I think, the right epithet – was with us for months on end, and through it one could distinguish a more biotic flavour – the stink of corrupting human flesh.

Landmarks no longer existed and it was difficult for troops to locate their positions or objectives. The British generally occupied low-lying land and troops were continually exposed to enemy fire. Rationing was almost impossible and water was scarce.

Haig overruled his senior officers' advice that the attack should be cancelled and it went ahead with disappointing results, although a few thousand prisoners were taken and the villages of Beaumont Hamel and Beaucourt were captured. The role of 31st Division in the final phase of the battle was to hold the far left of the line covering an attack by 3rd Division on Serre. The Second Pals were not required to 'go over the top' but suffered severe casualties on 13 November from heavy shellfire. The Battalion War Diary account for 13 November reads:

Battalion held line during attack on Serre and German lines further south, whilst 2 battalions of 92 Brigade attacked on our front to cover attack further south. 5.45 am Zero hour. Bombardment commenced punctually. Morning very misty, preventing observation…. Casualties for 13th – OR 13 killed, 21 wounded.

George's account for 13, 14 and 15 November provides detail of the attack and its aftermath:

13 November 1916 – Terrific bombardment commenced at 5.45 am when attack opened. 92nd Brigade (East Yorks) went over later and reached German second line – their objective. German prisoners began dribbling in – in tens and altogether 100 came in. Germans shelling Hébuterne heavily and causing casualties. East Yorks came back at

4 pm owing to 3rd Division falling back from Serre.

14 November 1916 – Germans shelling our line all day causing many casualties. Left the trenches at 6 pm and arrived back at Coigneux 10.30 pm after the most awful journey I have ever had.

15 November 1916 – Got up at 10 am but still tired. The boys are in a very bad state owing to being up to the waist in mud for 3 days. Saw Willie and he is in good health.

Although Serre village was entered by troops of 3rd Division, the outcome was the same as on 1 July with the British troops encountering uncut wire, violent barrages on no-man's land and stiff German defences. Many of the men lost their bearings in the fog and smoke and, in retiring, faced German counter-attacks, which infiltrated behind them and left them with no option but to surrender. By the afternoon, it was obvious that the attack had failed and not a yard of ground was won that day. It was not until the deliberate German withdrawal to the Hindenburg Line in February 1917 that the pile of rubble which was the remaining vestige of Serre village fell into British hands.

The Battle of the Somme ended on 19 November, which coincidentally was George's twenty-second birthday. The day brought some light relief from the arduous conditions:

Received birthday cake from Carrie (sister of his girlfriend, Lily). Celebrated my 22nd birthday at night – 5 bottles of champagne and a bottle of port which the Colonel gave us. Splendid party and Jackie (Sgt Mallett) and Cyril got drunk. Bed 12.30 am.

The next day he rose: *Tired but still cheerful. Left Coigneux and marched to Bayencourt (about 2 kilos). Got into a very nice billet. Shelling is quietening down.*

The end of the battle of attrition could not come soon enough. Both sides were exhausted and the weather, plus stubborn German resistance, had effectively signalled the end of the Somme campaign. Haig's decision to persist with the October and November attacks remains controversial to this day. His supporters would say that the policy of attrition had worked and the cream of the German Army had been destroyed, but others maintain that a casualty list of more than 400,000 was far too high a price to pay for limited territorial gains in an area of the Western Front which had little or no strategic importance. There was also mounting public concern at the level of casualties, seen in the reaction to the film *Battle of the Somme*, which during the autumn of 1916 was watched by more than 20 million people. For the first time, the population saw in graphic detail the cost of industrialised warfare.

13

HÉBUTERNE AND LEAVE,
20 NOVEMBER – 27 DECEMBER 1916

How they crowded the barns with lusty laughter,
Hailed the pierrots and shook each shadowy rafter,
Even could ridicule their own sufferings,
Sang as nothing but joy came after.

'POETICAL INTERPRETATIONS', BY EDMUND BLUNDEN, 1928

Fighting did not end on 19 November and the period after the battle saw frequent spells of trench duty in dreadful conditions with harassing artillery fire from the enemy who could not be certain that the British had called a halt to their offensive.

The Second Pals returned to front line duty in Hébuterne on 27 November. George's preoccupation with finding a safe dugout while in the trenches is seen in his diary entries for 27 and 28 November:

27 November 1916 – Went into the line again opposite Gommecourt Park. Our Headquarters in Hébuterne and the dugout is a splendid little place although fairly conspicuous from above.

28 November 1916 – Fritz sending his daily hate over but he is well to the left. Very little seems to be coming in this direction which is something to be thankful for.

The battalion Medical Officer, Dr McTavish showed similar concerns and wrote to his friend:

I'm writing this in an old cellar about 150 yards from our old friend Fritz across the way – at one time there was a house above us but now 'Na Poo - Fini' and my office is a 'ole – I don't know of a better one to go to.

His amusing reference to the famous Bruce Bairnsfather cartoon probably hides his real feelings and, indeed, there was no escape from the constant bombardment, such as the one described in the Battalion War Diary entry for 27 November:

Enemy sent whizzbangs at intervals during afternoon. Hébuterne heavily shelled with 5.9s and 4.2, both HE and shrapnel. Kellerman Trench and junction of Kellerman and Thorpe were heavily shelled, about 100 shells coming over altogether. Our artillery fairly quiet. Enemy artillery active up to midnight. TMs fairly active. Our 18 pdrs fired from 1.45 am to 2.30 am along enemy's front line. Heavy artillery retaliated on Puisieux with incendiary shell for enemy fire on Hébuterne during 27th.

The War Diary notes that during the month of November sixty soldiers were admitted to hospital due to sickness, which was, no doubt, caused by the severe impact of the weather and trench conditions. Many men, who had to stand for days on end in cold, waterlogged trenches, suffered from 'trench foot', which if untreated could lead to gangrene and the loss of toes or even foot and leg amputation. The army went to great lengths to ensure the men kept their feet dry with daily foot inspections by platoon commanders and regular supplies of socks and whale oil. Battalion Order Number 44 dated 2 December 1916 stated:

Company Commanders are responsible that every man goes to the dugout allotted for that purpose and changes his socks and dries and rubs his feet at least every 24 hours. Arrangements will be made at Battalion HQ for drying socks etc.

The neglect of feet was a disciplinary offence but efforts often came to naught when changing footwear under fire was near impossible and even a few hours of exposure could lead to the onset of the condition.

The men were also vulnerable to 'trench fever', the symptoms of which were similar to influenza or typhus with the illness beginning with a bad headache, exhaustion and a high temperature. Later on intense skin pains developed so that the patient could hardly bear the weight of bedclothes. Recovery from the fever was usually rapid, within four or five days, but its cause – excretions from trench lice – was not discovered until 1918. More regular access to bathhouses and laundries would have reduced the scale of the problem but the battlefield conditions on the Somme in late 1916 meant that this was not always possible. Shell shock was an ever-present feature of life in the front line and at first the army was slow to diagnose the condition and recognise its impact.

Following the end of the offensive, the immediate task of the army was to improve the defences of the ground taken and to repair the damage done to the lines of communication. This was a herculean task requiring new rail and road systems and a more serviceable trench network. Thousands of trench pumps were provided, construction materials brought forward and a huge salvage effort made to recover the vast mass of weapons and material scattered over the pulverised battlefield.

The rest offered by the brief periods in reserve was welcomed by the troops but this was not always a comfortable business, as illustrated by Dr McTavish who, in a letter to a friend, made the valid point that time in the trenches, contrary to views at home, was not a day-to-day, hand-to-hand struggle with the enemy:

> Very often we are in trenches where the mud and water is to our waists but that's only for two days, then two days of kind of half rest, then two days more. As for shooting Fritz, there are boys out here who have never fired a single shot in three months – what's the point of shooting when you can't see anything to shoot and the only time you see Fritz is when you make an advance and get into his front line – well that doesn't happen every day.

George's diary entries for 3 to 6 December also reveal that time spent at rest in the relative safety of their billets was a mixed blessing:

> 3 December 1916 – Relief arrived at noon and we set off on the dreary march to Rossignol Farm. Arrived there at 2.30 pm and found Walter cooking our tea. Went to bed early – quite 'jiggered'.

> 4 December 1916 – Had a rest so felt considerably better. Once more in this gloomy hole which is enough to give anyone the creeps. Refereed in a rugby match – absolute failure.

Rossignol Farm. 'This gloomy hole is enough to give anyone the creeps.' Rossignol Farm provided billets for the Pals during the closing stages of the Battle of the Somme when they experienced bad weather and atrocious trench conditions. Although only a short distance from the front line, it had not been badly hit by the German guns.

5 December 1916 – Walter and I had a day off so we walked to Doullens (14 miles) and spent the day there. It was splendid to see civilisation again and quite worth the long walk. Rode back in a bus and arrived at the farm 9 pm.

6 December 1916 – Once more resumed work but was pretty miserable owing to the beastly weather. Nothing but mud wherever you go. Cyril went to Couin to see the 'Popoffs'.

Over the years Rossignol Farm has changed little and it manages to look gloomy to this very day. Cyril Burgoyne's visit to the nearby village of Couin was to see the 94 Brigade Field Ambulance concert party, the 'Popoffs'. The battalion returned to front line duty at Hébuterne on 9 December and George was immediately called into action:

Went into trenches once more and in getting in got wet through. Pouring down. Went with Mr Bowden to bring in a German deserter who was coming across no-man's-land. Got him to H.Q. after a bit of a struggle.

The Battalion War Diary account, which appears to be written in George's hand, states:

About 12.30 pm an enemy deserter was seen approaching our lines along Gommecourt–Hébuterne Road. He was taken into custody and found to be under the influence of drink. An escort took him to Brigade.

The Pals held the line until 15 December, a period which saw the usual daily exchanges of artillery and mortar fire. George describes the nature of defensive warfare:

10 December 1916 – Artillery on both sides fairly active although as usual Bosche receiving most of it. Improvement in weather and it is a beautiful moonlit night.

11 December 1916 – Hell's bother all day. Bosche playing smash in Hébuterne. This morning 8 German aeroplanes over Hébuterne dropping bombs and directing fire. Very warm day indeed although we got nothing nearer than 100 yards.

12 December 1916 – Much quieter than yesterday although Hébuterne was shelled intermittently. We had a trial alarm at night and everything went off A1. I expect the old Bosche would be very much surprised.

13 December 1916 – Fritz paying attention to our district again but no particular damage done. The boys in advanced posts having a rotten time and almost up to the waist in mud and water.

14 December 1916 – Quieter during the day but in the evening our artillery got busy. Fritz retaliated with about 6 rounds our way and at the time of writing our artillery is paying them back about 20 to 1 (9 pm).

15 December 1916 – Day of relief and jolly glad too. Durhams came in about noon and we got out about 2 pm. Extremely pleased when we got to Sailly where we were billeted. Splendid room for Orderly Room.

The Battalion War Diary details the various artillery exchanges, including the attack by German aircraft on 11 November: '*an enemy aeroplane dropped four bombs onto and around a billet blowing in a cellar*'.

On 22 December George noted with some excitement: '*Expecting to go on leave any time now and consequently I am anxious for everything to go right.*' Army leave arrangements were somewhat haphazard, poorly and often unfairly administered and, of course, subject to the overriding needs of the army. The soldier's basic leave entitlement was ten days leave each year but this included the time spent travelling. The precise times given in George's diary show that he must have been acutely conscious that every hour on the journey was one hour less at home and also to be late back from leave was a serious military offence.

The precious leave warrant arrived at 7.30 pm on 23 December and fifty-two hours later he arrived home in Batley. His account of the closing days of 1916 is in marked contrast to what had gone before:

23 December 1916 – Waiting all day for warrant which arrived at 7.30 pm. Hurried to Acheux station and caught the 10 pm train. Stopped at Candas and spent the night in a

YMCA hut. Having a beastly time.

24 December 1916 – Left Candas at 8 am and started crawling towards Boulogne where we arrived at 4 pm. Went into Calais and got there 9 pm. Went into YMCA and spent the night there.

25 December 1916 – Left Calais at 10.35 am and arrived at Folkestone and then went on to London which we reached at 4 pm. Left London at 5 pm and arrived home 11.30 pm. Received a great welcome.

26 December 1916 – Went to see Mrs Armitage and in the afternoon went to watch Dewsbury and Batley. Batley won 8-0. At night took Lily and Betty to the Empire.

27 December 1916 – Went up to Cleckheaton to see Mrs Oddy. Spent the best part of the day there and arrived home 6.30 pm. Saw Mrs Ferrari. Went down to Lily's. Got a beastly cold and can scarcely speak.

The snail like ninety-mile rail journey to Calais took more than twenty-four hours and the entire journey from Sailly to Batley fifty-two hours. He slept in YMCA accommodation at Candas (near Amiens) and Calais while en route. The YMCA operated more than 300 rest and refreshment facilities in France and Flanders, staffed mainly by women volunteers. Some of the YMCA huts were to be found in front line areas and although they were generally out of the range of the guns, several YMCA workers were killed in aircraft raids or died of illness. They are buried alongside servicemen in the military cemeteries with the same type of headstone. The Salvation Army, the Church Army and the Catholic Church operated similar facilities. George found that they were not all were of the highest quality but does not say what caused his caustic comment that he was having a beastly time.

His arrival home in Batley must have been a great relief and his warm welcome well received. His first visit on Boxing Day was to Willie Armitage's mother, after which he went to the traditional Boxing Day Rugby League fixture between Dewsbury and Batley. Batley's victory (eight points to nil) was watched by 4,000 spectators at the Dewsbury Crown Flatts ground. The theatre visit in the evening with girlfriend, Lily, and sister,

Betty, was to the Dewsbury Empire where the variety programme featured a magician, a Lancashire stand-up comedian, an Indian rubber man, a chanteuse, a comedy double act, a musical trio and a troupe of tumblers. It would be intriguing to know how the show compared with the 'Popoffs' of Couin.

George's visits to Mrs Oddy and Mrs Ferrari on 27 December were to families who had sons serving in France with the Yorkshire Regiment and KOYLI. Great War soldiers were noted for their reticence in talking about their experiences and George was no exception. He no doubt reassured the families that their sons were well but it is unlikely that he said much else. His diary, carried safely from France, would have been placed in the hands of either Lily or his family, and after reading his story they would have been able to reach their own conclusions about the nature of the war. Given the year's events and the narrow scrapes he survived, his final diary entry for the year, written on 27 December, '*got a beastly cold and can scarcely speak*', seems somewhat ironic.

While George was on leave, the battalion was out of the line and the Battalion War Diary entries amount to barely half a dozen lines with the only notable comment that on Christmas Day trench working parties were suspended. In a letter to his friend, Dr McTavish gave a lively account of the battalion's move to the rest area at Couin and the season's festivities:

Well now for Xmas. We were very lucky to be out of the front line – we were back in rest billets, just far enough away to hear all the noise and yet not be a part or parcel of it. We were about three miles back and for the most of the time as safe as we were back thirty miles. Old Fritz only shells places that far back periodically, he may leave you quite alone for weeks and then all of a sudden he takes a notion and throws iron rations at you. He does everything the same – by method as it were – if he starts shelling a place he makes it hot while it lasts – if one shell comes over you can take it for granted that more will follow all about the same place. Or else he will start at one end and drop a shell every fifty yards all along the trench. He will never do anything by 'the any old way will do' style and has a method for everything and always follows it.

Well I'm getting away from Xmas. We got out of the trenches the evening of the 23rd so it left us a wee while to get things fixed up. We were all billeted in huts, nice brand new ones – the only trouble was they were cold – and nothing to warm them except what you can make in the way of a stove out of two tin cans.

We were very busy decorating the hut – Headquarters Mess – we got a Xmas tree – had it decorated – and presents for each officer in the battalion hung on it. Some got tin whistles, trumpets etc and a small present from the CO for each in the shape of a knife or small pair of scissors. We had all the walls decorated with holly and Chinese lanterns hung about. Even the mistletoe was there – the only thing missing was the girl! And as we had dipped down in our pockets and had bought enough oranges, dates, figs, nuts and apples for every man in the battalion, we were all happy for Xmas Eve. While we were having dinner the band was playing outside our hut. All of a sudden singing started so we went out to see – about 40 of the Tommies were there singing Christmas carols. The Colonel was so tickled he headed the procession and took them and the band over to serenade the Divisional General; then to one of the Field Ambulances and to the headquarters of the Divisional Artillery. Everybody quite enjoyed it.

On Christmas Day all officers and men enjoyed a Christmas dinner followed by sports and a concert in the evening in a large barn holding 800 or 900 men. Dr McTavish remarked that at the officers' dinner that night there were only four officers left out of the twenty-two who had been present at the Christmas meal in Egypt the previous year and although the dinner went well, according to Dr McTavish:

It wasn't nearly as wild as we had in Egypt for that was one I'll never forget – still we had a good time. I don't suppose the boys who were actually in the front line did quite as well.

14

HÉBUTERNE AND THE GERMAN RETREAT, 1 JANUARY – 18 MARCH 1917

So 1917 started lucky for me – both the Company HQ and the Battalion HQ have been blown to bits since – but we were not there.

FROM A LETTER TO A FRIEND, DR GEORGE BOYD MCTAVISH,
MEDICAL OFFICER 18TH WEST YORKSHIRE REGIMENT

George made no mention of keeping any other wartime diaries and although it is clear from his diary that he corresponded frequently with his family and friends, there are no surviving letters or cards. His army service records were among the 70 per cent of soldiers' records lost in the London Blitz in September 1940 when the War Office records store in London was destroyed by fire. The details of his service from January 1917 to his discharge in June 1919 therefore rely on a small number of personal and official documents, Battalion War Diaries, newspaper articles in the Batley local press and personal accounts, such as when he told me that he had been present at the death of his '*three best friends*' (see Chapter 15).

His return from leave cannot have been easy and the battalion spent the first few days of the New Year under heavy shellfire in the trenches at Hébuterne. The perils of men exposed to the daily routine of artillery attack are described vividly by Dr McTavish in his account of the dangers he faced in making his way from one of the Company Headquarters to Battalion Headquarters on New Year's Day:

Two or three times I nearly got an iron ration from Fritz. I was going from one of our Company Headquarters to Battalion HQ. I had the option of two ways so I started out but hadn't gone very far when a shell burst about 150 yards ahead of me. Well it being the New Year and the first day, I must have been nervous for I turned around and started back to go the other way. Well I didn't know it then but I do now that if I hadn't done so, I wouldn't have been here to tell the tale for I had only gone back 20 yards when another shell hit plumb in the path and just where I would have been if I had gone on. Well, as I said, I turned back, started the other way and this time a shell hit the foot of a tree about 100 yards in front of me. I stopped for a second then went on, for old Fritz never sends two shells one immediately after the other. He always allows a few seconds. So I thought if he does, I will be far enough past. I then had to go through a gap in some barbed wire entanglements and only got about 30 yards past when a shell hit right in the gap and left a hole six feet deep and 10 feet across – just where I'd been a few moments before. It covered me with dirt but no iron rations. So I picked myself up – laughed – and went on. So 1917 started lucky for me – both the Company HQ and the Battalion HQ have been blown to bits since – but we were not there.

Relief from front line duty came on 10 January 1917 when 93rd Brigade moved to the Doullens area for a month in reserve, resting and being trained in a newly introduced platoon system. Experience of the Somme offensive showed that the infantry needed to move more quickly and flexibly in small, mixed-arm teams with greater fire power and heavier weapons, such as the Lewis Gun, a portable light machine gun which could, if necessary, be operated by one man. The Battalion War Diary describes the training:

Battalion commenced training in accordance with new system of platoon organisation under which platoon and Company officers are entirely responsible for the training of their units, including bombers and Lewis gunners and rifle grenadiers. Work principally devoted to setting-up drill, platoon drill, musketry and reorganisation of platoons, together with route marches. Only half each day devoted to work, the remainder (alternately morning and afternoon by half battalions) to recreation – football, running, tug-of-war, bayonet fighting, bomb throwing and boxing – in which all men took part.

Dr McTavish's account of this period details the type of duties he carried out when the battalion was in rest behind the lines:

Just at present we are far back of the firing line getting a month's rest after nine long months of front line work. The boys are enjoying themselves. Of course they have a lot of training to do but half the day they spend at compulsory sports. Everybody has to do something – either play football, tug of war, bomb throwing, cross country running, boxing or some such thing. No spectators allowed except your humble servant of course. This was my programme for yesterday; up in the morning at 7 am – saw the sick, lame, lazy and sinful ones; had breakfast at 8.30 am – visited billets to see they were nice and tidy; had lunch, went for a ride on my little horse which by the way is the best little horse in sunny France. Got back at 3 pm and went to see a football match against another battalion. We won. Came back. Had tea. Went to see a sick civilian – an old man – then to see an old lady who fell and broke two of her ribs. Fixed her up and then visited the Field Ambulance. Next had dinner and after that I went to bed. Today I'm to have tea with the Mayoress to meet her daughters. What an ordeal! Still I hear she speaks English fairly well, so it may help out a wee bit but I was never struck on 'teas'. I look on them very much as a punishment.

After a break of six weeks, the Pals returned to the trenches on 21 February 1917. Once more the battalion held the line at Hébuterne opposite Rossignol Wood where they were met by desultory exchanges of artillery fire. On 23 February the Battalion War Diary reported unusual activity in the enemy trenches:

A fire was observed in enemy line … the smoke ascending as if a dugout was on fire. Artillery was informed and 18 pdrs fired continually for several hours. A good deal of movement was observed at this point.

The fire marked the start of the German withdrawal to the newly constructed Hindenburg Line. By straightening their line between Arras in the north and Soissons in the south, a distance of nearly 60 miles, the Germans needed thirteen fewer divisions to man this part of the front, thereby making good some of their losses on the Somme. The Germans had skilfully kept their retreat a secret but early signs of movement, such as the unexplained smoke from their trenches, betrayed their intentions. At 11pm on 24 February, 93rd Brigade Headquarters, suspecting that the enemy was evacuating his trenches ordered platoon-size patrols to be sent out to investigate. The Battalion War Diary reported:

11 pm – Brigade wired that enemy was thought to be evacuating his lines opposite V Corps front and ordered patrols to be pushed out to investigate. Two patrols of one platoon each to be sent by us. Company Commanders summoned to Battalion HQ and given instructions as to operations.

In the event eight platoons, comprising some 300 men, were ordered to move forward with a zero hour of 4.30 am on 25 February. The Battalion War Diary continues:

3 am – Notified Company Commanders that zero would be 5 am.

3.15 am – Message received from Brigade that if enemy line unoccupied, patrols were to push forward to objectives and act with vigour.

6.40 am – 'B' Company reported bomb and rifle fire on each flank.

6.43 – Enemy artillery commenced to be active.

6.52 am – Lieut Thornton ('A' Coy) reported to be on first objective but not in touch with 'C' Coy.

7.10 am – 2/Lt Hartman (19th Divisional Arty) reported at Battalion HQ that Lieut Thornton had gained the tongue of the salient and Lieut Sleigh was moving through the wood. A party of 10 Bosche had been seen on the left and dispersed with Lewis gun fire. Reported this to Brigade.

The clearing of Rossignol Wood took almost a week and proved to be a costly business as the Germans employed strong 'stay behind' parties with covering artillery to delay the British advance. Although the platoon raids were successful in establishing the state of the German defences, it needed a full-scale effort by several battalions, including both battalions of the Bradford Pals, to capture the wood. Enemy strong points, manned by machine-gun teams and thick belts of barbed wire had to be overcome as the men inched forward to capture their objectives.

As part of his duties, Dr McTavish went forward with the attacking troops and his account reveals the excitement of a successful advance and some of the risks involved:

Well the next few days and nights were rather strenuous – still we had a real good time. We were chasing Fritz out of a line he had held since he sat down in 1914. We took or at least occupied a wood that he had held with machine guns. We sent patrols out. Most of them came back with good reports. We had strong patrols out and a little later we got word we owned the wood. I went over right away and the rest of the battalion followed. I had picked out a dugout to live in and put a notice up to the effect that I owned the home and then went scouting around to see what I could find. When I came back I found two guards on my abode. I said, 'Well what are you doing?' 'Oh we belong to the party that are watching the dugouts to see that no Germans come out. Our orders are that if we hear a noise we are to throw these bombs down.' I replied, 'Oh I see, I'm glad you didn't come while I was down there.' The joke was that I had got ahead of our search party. Still if I hadn't come out when I did the joke would have been on me. The next day we took two more of Fritz's lines and two strong points. In one we got 24 prisoners and two machine guns. It was real nice to see Fritz coming out with his hands up.

The two Pals battalions suffered more than 200 casualties in the capture of the wood, the majority being from the First Bradford Pals, some of whom were taken prisoner by the enemy after coming under heavy machine-gun fire. Controversy surrounded the actions of one body of soldiers who were missing, believed captured. After a lengthy investigation, the Fifth Army Commander reached the conclusion that a party of sixteen men from the First Bradford Pals led by a Sergeant had deserted. Perhaps the most damning evidence came from Private Walter Higgins of 'A' Company of the First Pals whose statement reads:

I went into action on the morning of the 27th February with my platoon, No 4, under the command of Sergeant Farrar. We took cover as soon as the German Machine Guns opened fire. A heavy fire was kept up and it was practically impossible to move. At about 8 am a party on my left of three or four men crawled out and put up their hands and shouted 'Kamerad' and 'Adolph' and ran towards the German lines without their rifles. The Germans then ceased fire and about 18 more men went over from my left. About half an hour afterwards I heard voices from the rear which I did not recognise saying,

'Come on let's get up both together.' Three men then came towards me with their hands up shouting 'Kamerad'. They asked me to go with them. I refused to do so; they then walked straight into the German lines. I do not know the names of any of the men I saw going across. They were all men of the new draft and I do not know any of them. I did not see any NCOs going across. All the NCOs of my platoon were killed or wounded. I remained in the same position until 4 pm. I saw seven or eight men lying on the ground either killed or wounded.

The action of the men who deserted certainly seems reprehensible but the practice of sending new drafts straight into action, without any battlefield acclimatisation or tactical training, says much for the regard senior staff had for the welfare and fighting efficiency of their men. Following the incident, the uncompromising message sent from Headquarters to all 31st Division troops bears witness to the harshness of discipline in the British Army:

It should be made known to all ranks that if men are seen going over to the enemy they should be fired on at once, and that men who surrender without sufficient reason or desert to the enemy, will be tried after the war and shot.

On 2 March, after the wood had been cleared of the enemy, two companies of the Second Bradford Pals were tasked with *'digging graves and collecting as many bodies as possible'*. (Battalion War Diary) The map coordinates indicate that the graves were to be dug on the southwest edge of Rossignol Wood where Owl Trench Military Cemetery now stands. The cemetery is overlooked by the brooding presence of Rossignol Wood. Fifty officers and men of the First Bradford Pals are buried in a mass grave.

Shortly after the action, Dr McTavish left the battalion suffering from a serious chest infection, possibly pneumonia, which was common among men suffering from exhaustion and life in and around the trenches. He was sent to a military hospital on the coast, probably at Wimereux, just to the north of Boulogne. In a letter from hospital to his friend he describes two different views of 'Blighty':

I look out of my window across the channel – on clear days I see the white cliffs of Dover. To me they mean Britain – that's all I know that they are part of the little islands that rule the world and more at this present moment than ever before in history. But to the Tommy an altogether different feeling – to him it is 'Blighty' – no matter how badly they are wounded, or how slight, the question they always ask is not 'will I lose my arm or leg or maybe both – or will it get better or is it bad' – no, not a bit of it. There is only one question – 'Will I get to Blighty?'

When 'Mac', as he was known to the Pals, recovered, he was posted to 99th Field Ambulance, attached to 33rd Division. In September 1918, in the attack on the Hindenburg line at Villers Guislain, he won a second bar to his Military Cross for recovering and treating wounded soldiers under fire. Part of his citation reads:

Although gassed, he still carried on, and saved the life of an officer who was knocked over by a shell when he was talking to him, holding an artery until help came, he himself having been knocked over by the same shell.

Coincidentally, this action occurred at the same time and within a mile of where George's brother, Tom, won his Military Medal. Following the Armistice, Dr McTavish served with the armed forces in China until 1920 when he returned to practice in North Winnipeg. During Second World War, he served as District Medical Officer in Winnipeg and also worked for the Department of Veteran Affairs. He died in 1965 aged eighty-two, survived by his wife, daughter and three sons.

After the capture of Rossignol Wood, the Pals spent the middle two weeks of March in the neighbourhood of Hébuterne, helping to restore the defences on their part of the front. The Second Pals War Diary describes the provision of working parties to lay tram and railway tracks. From 8–12 March virtually the entire battalion (fourteen officers and 500 men), under the supervision of 268 Railway Company, was engaged in laying a track for a broad gauge railway at Euston Dump. The KOYLI Pioneer (Miners) Battalion were occupied with the recovery of ground that had been occupied by the Germans where they had to take great care to avoid booby traps left by the enemy. According to Captain Ede England:

Every imaginable device was used by the enemy. A bayonet would be stuck in the ground, and its withdrawal would cause a violent explosion. To step on the stairway of a deep dugout was the signal for complete destruction of the shelter. In the course of time, however, we became wise to almost all these traps.

On 18 March the Pals were placed *'under 4 hours notice to proceed East if necessary'* (Battalion War Diary). The battalion duly set off that day but in a different direction – heading north.

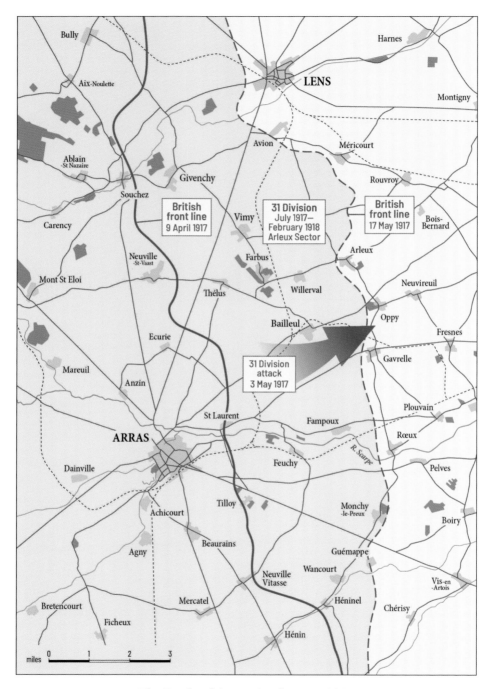

The Battle of Arras, April – May 1917

15

THE BATTLE OF ARRAS,
APRIL – JUNE 1917

The air is loud with death,
The dark air spurts with fire,
The explosions ceaseless are.
Timelessly now, some minutes past,
Those dead strode time with vigorous life,
Till the shrapnel called 'An end!'
But not to all. In bleeding pangs
Some borne on stretchers dreamed of home,
Dear things, war – blotted from their hearts.

FROM 'DEAD MAN'S DUMP' BY ISAAC ROSENBERG, WRITTEN IN 1917.
ROSENBERG WAS KILLED NEAR ARRAS IN APRIL 1918

On 25 March 1917, after a six-day march, the men of 31st Division reached the Béthune area where they commenced a programme of re-equipment and training in preparation for a major offensive which was to be launched at Arras. The Bradford Pals were housed in purpose-built accommodation at Feuillade Barracks in Béthune and spent the next three weeks on a variety of training schemes. On 15 April the battalions moved south to Frévillers, a small village 15 miles to the northwest of Arras where a further two weeks of specialist training was carried out, including tactical manoeuvres at Company level. By this time, the Pals can have been in little doubt about what their future held in store, for on Easter Monday, 9 April 1917, Sir Douglas Haig had launched an all-out attack on the nearby Vimy Ridge and the area to the east and south of the city of Arras. 31st Division featured in his plans to exploit the initial gains.

The decision to fight at Arras was ill-conceived. Haig, now promoted to Field

Marshal, had a strong preference for an attack in Flanders to the north but once more had to concede to French pressure for a joint attack at the juncture of the two armies. General Nivelle, the newly appointed Commander of the French Army, pinned his hopes on a war-winning breakthrough towards Saint-Quentin. The unexpected German withdrawal to the Hindenburg Line made Nivelle's plan redundant and he switched the focus of his attack to an assault on the heavily fortified ridge of the Chemin des Dames, 40 miles further to the south. In support of his ally, Haig agreed to a more limited attack at Arras on the northern extremity of the Hindenburg Line in the hope that he could break the German line and capture the town of Cambrai, an important rail hub.

The start of the Arras offensive went well with a brilliantly executed assault on Vimy Ridge by four divisions of Canadian and British troops who captured the commanding heights with relatively few casualties. Lessons learned on the Somme were put to good use. The use of several tunnels enabled the troops to launch their attacks much closer to the German line and the creeping barrage was better planned, allowing the attackers to surprise the enemy in his dugouts. Public acclaim for the success was so great that the Battle of Arras was often referred to as 'Vimy', even though much of the battle was to take place to the south of the ridge around the city of Arras itself. As well as success on Vimy Ridge, the first week of the battle saw significant gains to the east and south of the city but atrocious weather conditions, including snow, which left the trenches deep in mud and slush, forced Haig to postpone the immediate follow-up attacks.

The parallel French offensive on the Chemin des Dames, which started on 16 April, made limited progress on the first day but it soon became apparent that the German defences were far too strong to be breached. With more than 100,000 casualties in the first week alone and no worthwhile gains, the French High Command decided to halt the attack and Nivelle was relieved of his duties. The defeat sparked widespread mutinies among the French infantry who, while willing to defend their lines, refused to engage in any further major attacks. It was to be a year before the morale of the French Army was sufficiently restored to enable it to resume large-scale offensive operations, leaving the British to bear the brunt of the campaign in France.

On 28 April, in preparation for their part in the Battle of Arras, the Bradford Pals moved to hutments at Écoivres, adjacent to an airfield occupying a field below the ruined Abbey of Mont-Saint-Éloi, 4 miles behind Vimy Ridge. April 1917, which became known as 'Bloody April', was a torrid time for British aircrew who suffered severe

The Abbey of Mont-Saint-Éloi. On the eve of 31st Division's
3 May 1917 attack on the villages of Gavrelle and Oppy, the Bradford
Pals were billeted close to the ruined abbey of Mont-Saint-Éloi. A
squadron of Royal Navy Air Service scout planes was stationed in the
field below the abbey and one of the squadron pilots, 'Mad Major'
Draper, was noted for entertaining the troops by flying his plane
between the twin towers of the abbey.

losses. A maximum effort had to be made by the Royal Flying Corps reconnaissance squadrons to provide the army and its artillery with the best intelligence of enemy positions. Unfortunately, at this stage of the war the Royal Flying Corps found itself completely outclassed by the technically superior aircraft of the German Air Force with their brightly painted Albatros D.III scouts, led at Arras by Baron Richthofen and his 'Flying Circus'. In the month of April the RFC suffered more than 400 casualties and lost almost 300 aircraft, twenty-two of which fell to the guns of Richthofen, known popularly by both sides as the 'Red Baron' or in German propaganda as the 'Red Fighter Pilot'.

Despite their losses, the British squadrons stuck to their task and largely met their objectives. Some of the most effective opposition to the enemy came from the scout squadrons of the Royal Naval Air Service who flew Sopwith Triplanes and French-built Nieuport 17s from Écoivres. A number of the RNAS pilots flying with 6th and 8th Squadrons RNAS became 'Aces'. Perhaps the most colourful was 'Mad Major' Chris Draper who often flew between the twin towers of the ruined Abbey at Mont-Saint-Éloi to entertain the nearby troops. After the war he became a stunt pilot and actor, as well as a double agent in the 1930s. In 1953 he was arrested for flying under fifteen bridges of the river Thames but was let off with a caution and ten guineas costs.

Field Marshal Haig's immediate priority for the Arras offensive was to draw German troops away from the weakened and vulnerable French Army. Once again, Brigadier General Charteris, Chief of British Army Intelligence and Haig's 'Evil Counsellor', played a crucial role. He reported to Haig that the Germans had only ten reserve divisions on the Western Front and their battalion strengths were at dangerously low levels. This convinced Haig and the politicians at home that the enemy front could be broken at Arras and that the offensive should continue. Some of Haig's Generals were of the view that the same results could be achieved by the use of intense artillery barrages and no major infantry assaults. They felt that this would have been enough to keep the Germans guessing and reluctant to move their divisions to the Chemin des Dames front.

Haig pressed on throughout April and the infantry assaults which he ordered became known as the Second and Third Battles of the Scarpe, named after the river which flows through the region. The task of 31st Division and its Pals battalions was to secure the village of Gavrelle, which was partly in British hands and then capture the neighbouring village of Oppy. These villages were some 6 miles northeast of the Arras city centre. The Pals left their billets at Écoivres on 29 April and after an arduous six-hour march, went into the front line at Gavrelle in the early hours of 30 April. They were immediately greeted by a heavy artillery barrage, including gas and tear gas shells directed from a German observation balloon some 2 miles away. The Pals lost three dead and sixteen wounded in the shelling, a foretaste of what was to come.

The detailed planning of the 31st Division attack was complicated by disagreement about the merits of a night attack and how the battalions should be positioned at zero hour. It was not until 7.10 pm on 2 May that Brigade Operational Order 106 was received at Battalion Headquarters giving a zero hour of 3.45 am the next day. During the night the men moved into position in no-man's land, no easy feat given the darkness and the need to keep in touch with units on either flank. At 10.30 pm Second Lieutenant Dams and Second Lieutenant Bowden, who with George had captured the drunken deserter, bravely laid out tapes in no-man's land for the attacking troops to follow.

The covering British barrage commenced as planned at 3.45 am and the Pals launched their attack. According to the Battalion War Diary, the enemy artillery replied almost immediately. No-man's land was bathed in moonlight and the Germans, expecting an attack, had withdrawn most of their troops from the front line, enabling their artillery to catch the Pals in the open or in their own vacated trenches. This led to great confusion, as evidenced by the Battalion War Diary report of the actions of Second Lieutenant Harris, 'A' Company. Timed at 5.51 am, it reads:

> *After barrage had commenced, the Company became somewhat disorganised, and after crossing the road, the 16th and 18th West Yorks men and men of different Companies were mixed together. A great number congregated in a trench and himself and a 16th officer went over to their right and got 10 prisoners. The 16th officer then received information that they were being surrounded on both flanks. A party of the 16th were seen on the left & he took his men across with the prisoners. He saw OC 16th West Yorks there who said he had better report at Battalion H.Q. He did so and had now about 20 men and a Sgt with him.*

Other reports of confusion and heavy casualties flooded into the Battalion Headquarters, as the War Diary records:

6.13 am – Runners brought verbal message from CSM Nicholson, 'D' Company – all officers missing, majority of men casualties and he himself wounded. Runners said they got to enemy first line and were making to second line but a machine gun on either flank caused heavy casualties and then commenced to work round their rear.

6.52 am – 2/Lt Dams reported at Btn H.Q. With about 10 men he had got into enemy first line but enemy held second in strength. They had made a few prisoners but enemy counter-attacked in numbers & they were driven out. He was made a prisoner but got away. Enemy held trench near to WINDMILL. Our barrage was good; enemy put a barrage behind them. He thought the enemy aeroplane which flew low over our lines as they were forming up must have seen them as enemy seemed prepared.

Lieutenant Colonel Carter made desperate attempts to re-establish communications with the attacking companies and Brigade Headquarters, including the use of carrier pigeons but it was clear that the attack had failed and by noon the priority had switched to constructing a defensive line against possible enemy counter-attacks. This was successfully achieved and by night-time conditions were '*comparatively quiet*' with the survivors back at their starting point in their own front line trenches.

The German Air Force made frequent low level air attacks in support of their hard-pressed infantry, which in turn were countered with machine gun and Lewis gun fire. Low-level attacks against ground targets were extremely dangerous and the German Air Force attacks were not always successful. On 18 May the Battalion War Diary reported:

5.15 am – Enemy aeroplane flying low over our lines.

5.25 am – Enemy aeroplane brought down, red body, white wings, 2 black streamers, over support lines on right.

The downed aircraft with the red fuselage might have come from Baron Richthofen's squadron, as many of his pilots favoured the colour.

Both Pals battalions remained in the front line and support trenches at Gavrelle until 19 May, and were constantly shelled as the final stages of the Battle of Arras raged about them. On 18 May the Second Bradford Pals supported the Durham Light

Infantry in another night attack on Gavrelle and although they managed to reach their objectives, they were forced to retire as flanking units had no success in the face of German machine-gun fire and counter-attacks. On 19 May the two battalions were relieved by the Royal Naval Division and moved into rest at Écurie on the northern outskirts of Arras

The Pals casualty figures for the action at Arras were similar to those of 1 July 1916. Both first and second battalions lost more than 300 men and many of the dead could not be recovered due to the fighting having taken place on enemy held ground. The Second Pals War Diary report for the month of May lists a total of 329 casualties (including ten officers), of which thirty-three were killed, 132 missing and 164 wounded, including two self-inflicted wounds. Eighty-five per cent of the month's casualties were incurred on 3 May. The First Pals suffered 314 casualties.

The memorial at the Faubourg-d'Amiens Military Cemetery in the centre of Arras records the names of the 35,000 British troops who died in the Battle of Arras and have no known grave. The 'missing' of the Bradford Pals are listed there. Among George's papers are two photographs of a party of Imperial War Graves Commission staff posing in front of the memorial, designed by Edwin Lutyens, which was unveiled on 31 July 1932 by Viscount Hugh Trenchard, the former Commander of the Royal Flying Corps. The quality of the photographs is poor but George can be recognised in the group and it can be assumed that they had played a part in the construction of the memorial. It would not be surprising if he kept the images as a memento of the battle and the loss of so many of his comrades.

The Battle of Arras ended on 18 May 1917 with more than 150,000 British casualties. The daily casualty rate was the highest of any of the major British offensives, including the Somme and Third Ypres.

After May, the attention of Field Marshal Haig switched to Flanders where his longed-for offensive was being prepared. The fighting at Arras settled into the normal routine of artillery exchanges, sniping and patrols, both sides seeking to consolidate their defensive positions. Following a period of rest at Écurie and nearby Bray, the Bradford Pals returned to the Gavrelle sector on 15 June, where they were engaged in extensive repair work on the Gavrelle trenches. The Pals were subject to heavy artillery fire, one 5.9-inch shell hitting a trench and causing thirteen casualties. On 22 June they were relieved by the Leeds Pals and took up reserve positions about 3 miles behind the

Faubourg-d'Amiens Military Cemetery. George is second from left in the second row of Imperial War Graves Commission workers posing in front of the monument commemorating the flying services at the Fauberg-d'Amiens Military Cemetery in the centre of Arras. The memorial, designed by Sir Edwin Lutyens, lists the 35,000 missing at the Battle of Arras in 1917, and was unveiled by Marshal of the Royal Air Force Viscount Hugh Trenchard on 31 July 1932. It includes on its walls the names of the missing Bradford Pals who were killed in the attack on Gavrelle on 3 May 1917.

lines. The men were accommodated in dugouts and tents located in a railway cutting just to the north of the village of Saint-Laurent-Blangy.

The next day the Orderly Room tent was hit by a shell, killing George's close friends, Lance Corporal Cyril Burgoyne and Privates Walter Kellett and Sam Tweedale, and wounding Lieutenant Colonel Carter in the adjoining tent. The Battalion War Diary entry timed at 1 am states flatly:

Enemy shelled vicinity of camp with long range gun. One shell fell on Orderly Room tent killing three clerks and wounding Lt. Col Carter.

Reverend John Calderbank, the 93rd Brigade Padre met Lieutenant Colonel Carter the next day, who gave him the following account of the incident:

> *Three of the orderly room staff had been literally blown to pieces and he himself had had a miraculous escape. He had been sleeping in a tent next to the other men and although his tent was literally riddled with holes, and his British Warm which had been laid across his chest had been badly gashed, and his tunic full of holes, he had only received a small flesh wound.*

My father, when telling me about the incident, said that he had lost '*his three best friends*' and that shortly before the shell hit he had had the good fortune to have been '*sent on an*

Bailleul Road East Military Cemetery. 'My three best friends.' The three graves shown are of Lance Corporal Cyril Burgoyne and Privates Walter Kellett and Sam Tweedale who were killed on 23 June 1917 by a long-range shell while working in the Orderly Room tent. George had left the tent moments before the shell struck.

errand by the Colonel'. There is evidence from a Mallett family history website that 'Jackie' Mallett, the Orderly Room Sergeant, had also just left the tent and narrowly escaped the shell. Sergeant Mallett survived the war and returned to Bradford to manage the family firm which provided journalistic services to the wool trade.

This was the only occasion my father talked to me at any length about the war and the loss of such close colleagues must have had an enormous effect on him. All three men came from Bradford. Cyril Burgoyne, aged twenty-one, was a clerk in civil life and Walter Kellett, aged twenty-two, worked in an estate agent's office. The thirty-five-year-old Sam Tweedale, a grocer's clerk, was married with four daughters. Reverend Calderbank conducted the funeral service and the men are buried side-by-side in the Bailleul Road East Military Cemetery, not far from the railway cutting where the shell landed. The cemetery contains approximately 1,000 graves of which just over 500 are named. One commemorates Isaac Rosenberg, a Great War poet whose poem *Dead Man's Dump* was written at the time of the battle. He was killed in April 1918 at Fampoux, near Arras.

Directly across the road from the British cemetery is the German Military Cemetery of Saint-Laurent-Blangy, where 32,000 German soldiers who died in the Arras fighting are buried. Twenty-five thousand of these are in a single mass grave.

16

FAREWELL TO THE PALS,
JULY 1917 – FEBRUARY 1918

The severance of these Battalions from the Brigade is necessary in the interests of the whole Army, but that does not lessen the deep regret felt throughout all the remaining ranks of the Brigade. In times of hardship and danger, the 16th and 18th Battalions of the West Yorkshire Regiment have proved themselves brave, cheerful soldiers and good comrades.

SPECIAL BRIGADE ROUTINE ORDER DATED 11 FEBRUARY 1918

The details of George's army service after the middle of 1917 are sparse but information from his Discharge Certificate (Army Form Z21), Medal Cards and documents concerning his marriage in April 1918 to Suzanne Marguerite Levreux, a French girl from Rouen, provide an outline of where he served from mid-1917 to his demobilisation in June 1919. Battalion War Diaries are also of great help in providing detailed information about the military operations of the units to which he was attached.

The Bradford Pals remained in the Arras area from July 1917 to their disbandment in February 1918. Lieutenant Colonel Carter, having recovered from the wounds he had sustained on 23 June 1917, resumed command of the battalion on 3 August 1917. The Pals were deployed in the Acheville and Arleux-en-Gohelle sectors, 10 miles to the north of Arras and just south of the mining town of Lens. Gavrelle, where they had suffered grievously in May, was just 3 miles to the south.

From July 1917 to February 1918, 31st Division held a quiet part of the front, while Haig's major offensive to the north raged around the Messines Ridge and Ypres, culminating in the capture of Passchendaele village by the Canadians on 6 November 1917. During this period the Pals carried out the usual routine of alternating spells in the front line, in support and in rest. Artillery exchanges took their toll with the frequent use of gas by both sides.

The Second Pals distinguished themselves on 31 August by repelling a large German raiding party which was attempting to capture a section of trenches. Lieutenant Colonel Carter suspected a raid was in the offing after the Germans fired 1,000 shells at the Battalion Headquarters and support trenches. The Battalion War Diary account of the raid reads:

29 August 1917 – Enemy artillery extremely active. Approximately 1000 shells (4.2s, 5.9s and 77mm) fired around and in Battn HQ, and front and support lines heavily shelled on left.

30 August 1917 – 1 pm Orders issued to Companies for action in case of raid by enemy on our left, to which artillery activity pointed. Three daylight patrols, each 2 ORs, in sniper's suits, brought back useful intelligence as to enemy movements. Enemy is seen to leave front line trenches to move back to support line at day break.

31 August 1917 – Quiet night after 10 pm until 2.45 am (31st) when enemy put barrage on front and support lines on our left flank and attempted to raid our trenches with two parties about 50 strong in all. Parties were observed before reaching our wire and our Lewis guns broke them up. One wounded prisoner was taken; the enemy left several dead, including one officer. The captured material included one light machine gun, one Bangalore torpedo, 3 rifles, I gas respirator, 1 box machine gun ammunition.

The way the raid was handled was a great improvement from the bitter experience at Neuve-Chapelle in July the previous year when the battalion was caught unawares and eighty men of 'B' Company were lost to a German trench raid. Brigade and Corps staff sent complimentary messages, with the Corps Commander's message:

The Corps Commander has read with interest the report on the attempted raid of the 31st August and requests that you will convey his congratulations to the CO 18th West Yorks Regiment, and the troops under his command, on the accurate appreciation of the enemy's intentions and adequate steps to frustrate them and the confidence and promptitude displayed in meeting the attack.

Patrolling no-man's land was a frequent activity by both sides and the Battalion War Diary description two patrols in November is typical of the work on which the men were engaged:

10 November 1917 – Daylight patrol went out at 6.30 am returning at 11.00 am after reconnoitring enemy defences. Three machine guns located. Second daylight patrol examined enemy wire. Third daylight patrol worked south-east along Oppy–Arleux Road as far as Willows. Reported light trench mortar firing from SAP in front of enemy line behind Willows.

14 November 1917 – 1 NCO and 5 men took up a position in no man's land at 5.30 am under cover of mist. About 7.15 am sentry was seen with head and shoulders above parapet of enemy sap. Cpl Barker fired and man threw up his hands and disappeared groaning.

The winter of 1917/18 was extremely harsh and apart from desultory artillery exchanges there was little military action. The conditions are graphically described in the Battalion War Diary entry for the period 15 to 19 January 1918:

Owing to thaw and rain, the condition of the trenches became very bad, subsidence taking place & the bottom of the trenches becoming in places two or three feet or more deep in thick adhesive mud. Communication trenches became impassable and movement had to take place over the top. The posts were consequently isolated during day time. Visibility was very bad and there was exceedingly little activity on either side.

During the winter of 1917/18, the army carried out a major reorganisation of its infantry battalions in France with the number of battalions in each Division being reduced from twelve to nine, leaving each brigade with three battalions. The change was forced by severe shortages of front line manpower caused by the heavy casualties suffered in the major battles of 1917 and also by Prime Minister Lloyd George's reluctance to allocate additional manpower to the Western Front, which he thought Field Marshal Haig would waste in further costly and abortive attacks. Lloyd George made the point that the army had already received more than its fair share of precious manpower during

1917 and had enjoyed an increase of 300,000 in the total number of troops in France and Belgium. Lloyd George did not acknowledge that the actual number of front line fighting troops had reduced by 100,000 and against fierce opposition from the army Generals, who with good cause saw great risk from German reinforcements which were being redeployed from the Russian front, the Imperial War Cabinet – which had no military members – decided to proceed with the cuts.

The reductions fell almost entirely on Kitchener New Army battalions and between January and March 1918 115 battalions disappeared and some forty were merged with other battalions. The Bradford Pals battalions were not spared. News of disbandment was broken to the men of the Second Pals on 1 February 1918 at Bray Camp, near Écurie in the Arras area, when their Commanding Officer, Lieutenant Colonel Carter

addressed all officers and ORs of Battalion in Church Army Hut explaining reasons for disbanding of Battalion and his appreciation of the manner in which all ranks had worked under him. (Battalion War Diary)

The War Diary lists where the men were sent. Thirty-three officers and 720 men were transferred to nine other battalions of the West Yorkshire Regiment. The transport section of forty men, including their vehicles and animals, were attached to the 1st Brigade of Guards and the last batch of eight officers and forty-two men were instructed to proceed by rail to XIII Corps Reinforcement Camp at the village of Pernes, 10 miles west of Béthune. This group of men included Lieutenant Colonel Carter, Major Robinson, his Second-in-Command and the remaining members of the Battalion Headquarters and Orderly Room staff who were needed to arrange the transfer of the men and clear up the battalion's business. They would have certainly included George, and the War Diary entries for January and February are in his handwriting. The final Battalion War Diary entry, dated 15 February 1918, was signed by Lieutenant Colonel Carter and states simply: 'This reduced strength of unit in the Field to _NIL_.'

The disbandment of a battalion must have been keenly felt with the splitting up of friends and the loss of comradeship forged in the hardship and danger of battle. The fighting troops of the battalion had the consolation of moving with their officers in half-company groups to other West Yorkshire Regiments but the men from the Headquarters group would be scattered. So far as the last batch of men from Battalion Headquarters is concerned, there is no reference in the Battalion War Diary to the units to which they were sent once they had reached the reinforcement camp at Pernes.

In the battalion's twenty-five months of active service, twenty-four officers and 380 non-commissioned officers and men were killed in action or died of their wounds. Of these just over 200 were from the original volunteers. In the British Army the ratio of dead to wounded in the Great War was approximately 1:2, which would indicate that in addition to the 400 dead, another 800 men were wounded. The chance of death or injury was therefore very high and the surviving troops had still to face the bloodiest year of the war.

Suzanne Marguerite Levreux (1898–1979).
Suzanne, a nineteen-year-old engineer's daughter,
from Rouen, married George on 6 April 1918.
They had three sons – Cecil, Robert and Jacques
– prior to divorcing in 1936.

17

A WARTIME MARRIAGE,
APRIL 1918

*Permission to marry will not be granted unless the Commanding Officer has
satisfied himself as to the woman's character.*

THE KING'S REGULATIONS AND ORDERS FOR THE ARMY. HMSO 1914

On 6 April 1918 George married Suzanne Marguerite Levreux at the Anglican Church
of All Saints, Rouen. Suzanne was the nineteen-year-old daughter of a mechanic
('*mechanicien*'), Arsène Levreux and came from Rouen. The Reverend Chaplain, Samuel
Hemphill of the Colonial and Continental Church Society officiated. The society was
an agency of the Church of England and was responsible for overseas missions. Its
church in Rouen was founded in 1843 to care for the large number of British sailors and
railway workers who visited the city. The certificate of marriage gives the usual details
of residence, parents' names and those of the two witnesses, James Henry Shaw and
Suzanne's father, Arsène. George's profession is given as Sergeant, 18th Battalion West
Yorkshire Regiment, and the corresponding entry in the UK Foreign Overseas Register
of Marriages also states that he is a Sergeant. He received a card from the Orderly
Room Sergeants of the West Yorkshire Regiment, wishing him '*future happiness*' and the
marriage was reported in the *Batley News* in the following article:

Batley News – 20 April 1918
*A Batley soldier, Sergeant George William Broadhead 18th Battalion West Yorks, son of
Mr and Mrs A Broadhead, 89 Granville Terrace, Mount Street, Batley has found a bride
in France. The lady is Mademoiselle Suzanne Marguerite Levreux, Rue Traversière,
Rouen to whom he was married in the famous old French town on the 6th inst.*

His best man was Private James Shaw of Batley an old friend he met at Rouen.

Sergeant Broadhead is well known in Batley. Before joining the Army he was Head Clerk at the Corporation Electricity Works and previously had performed clerical duties at the Gas Works and in the Town Hall.

The twenty-six-year-old James Henry Shaw came from Healey in Batley and prior to his enlistment in 1915 had worked as a clerk in the Borough Treasurer's Department of Batley Corporation, where he would have been one of George's work colleagues. Jimmy, as he was known, was a member of the Army Service Corps and was attached to a Mechanical Transport unit, which may well have been based in Rouen.

We are left to wonder how George's 'old flame', Lily Parker, received the news of his marriage but it seems that they remained friends and in later life he visited the Parker family at their home in Dewsbury, my sister and I going with him. Lily died in 1968 at the age of seventy-three, still a spinster.

Wartime marriages to French women were not unusual, even though the army and the French authorities might not have encouraged them. As well as needing to satisfy the army of the suitability of his future wife, the twenty three year old George also needed to provide a character reference for himself. Among his private papers is a letter from Alderman J.W. Turner JP to the army authorities, dated 21 March 1918, which reads:

I have known Geo. W. Broadhead from his boyhood and watched his behaviour during the 7 years he was employed by the Batley Corporation. I have the utmost pleasure in testifying to his good character and all round ability. He was diligent, painstaking, well-mannered and showed a disposition to get on and do his best. He was trustworthy and gave general satisfaction.

John William Turner was a fifty-seven-year-old retired woollen rag merchant who was Mayor of Batley from 1901 to 1904. His family had been neighbours of the Broadhead family in Bunkers Lane, Staincliffe for many years before Armitage moved to Halifax Road, closer to the centre of Batley. Turner's imposing villa, 'Deighton Holme', was barely a stone's throw away from Bunkers Lane and Staincliffe Church and its school.

Suzanne was pregnant when she and George married and their first child, Cecil George Haslam Broadhead, was born on 30 October 1918 at the Levreux family home,

8 Rue Traversière, which was the address given for both bride and groom on the Certificate of Marriage. The family house, which still stands, is in a quiet back street about half a mile from the city centre, not far from the right bank of the river Seine.

Cecil's date of birth makes it likely that their relationship started towards the end of 1917 which raises the intriguing question of how a soldier serving with his battalion in the Arras sector was able to form a relationship with Suzanne from Rouen, more than 100 miles away. Although Suzanne may have been living or working away from home in 1917, George had reason to be in Rouen. He would not have taken leave there but to become an Orderly Room Sergeant, it was necessary to undertake specialist training in the role and many of the training schools were located in Rouen. Further evidence that he was away from his battalion in late 1917 comes from the entries in the Battalion War Diary for the whole of December 1917 and the first few days of 1918, which are written in an unusual, clumsy hand which is certainly not his.

At this stage of the war the army laid great emphasis on intensive training for key posts. Courses could last for up to five or six weeks, of which Charles Carrington in his

Lieutenant Colonel Herbert Carter (1886–1919). 'Colonel Carter came back from leave about 2 am and roused the whole place — particularly me.' Lieutenant Colonel Herbert Carter was the Commanding Officer of the 2nd Bradford Pals and the Orderly Room was an important element of his staff headquarters. He was wounded by the German shell which in June 1917 killed George's three Orderly Room colleagues. George may have been tempted to accompany Carter to Vladivostok in May 1918 to assist the White Russian army in its fight against the Bolsheviks.

memoir *Soldier from the Wars Returning*, gives an amusing account:

> *There was no end to one's military education. Schools of instruction in all technicalities and at all grades sprang up behind the front … sergeants and young officers were much exposed to educational treatment and if they had the greatest share of danger in the line, they enjoyed the prerequisites – now and then – of being 'sent on a course'. At least it would be safe and comfortable, at best it might be a mere holiday – a binge.*

It was unlikely that the happy couple had long together before military duties intervened. Following the disbandment of the Second Bradford Pals, transfer to a new unit was necessary and on 12 July 1918 George was posted to The London Regiment. His Discharge Certificate states that he served with 16th Battalion The London Regiment (Queen's Westminster Rifles), and the British War Medal roll (Army Form W.5102) gives service dates with The London Regiment of July 1918 to June 1919, following which he was discharged to the Army Reserve.

There is no record of the reasons why George was transferred to the London Regiment. He once said to me, and at the time I thought it was in jest, that he could not decide whether to stay in France, join the Black and Tans Militia in Ireland or enlist with the Allied forces supporting the White Russians in the civil war against the Bolsheviks. The dates of the Irish and Russian campaigns make these credible choices. Indeed, shortly after the disbandment of the Second Pals, its Commanding Officer, Lieutenant Colonel Carter, was posted to Vladivostok in Siberia as a British Army adviser where his Russian language skills, which he had acquired as a military attaché before the war, would have been of value. He died there of pneumonia in February 1919, aged thirty-three, shortly after the birth of his first child. Given George's close working relationship with his former Commanding Officer, it is possible that Carter tried to persuade him to accompany him to Russia as one of his personal staff. Perhaps wisely, his decision was to stay in France with the London Regiment and his new wife.

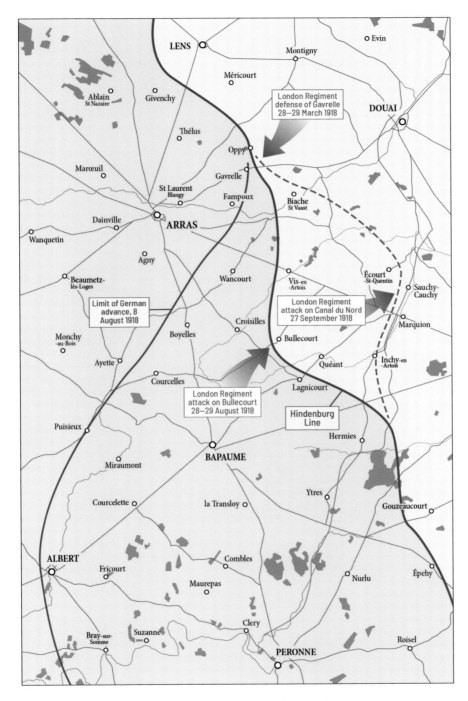

The London Regiment, March – September 1918

The Town Hall, Doullens. In June 1916, while behind the lines practising the attack for 1 July 1916, George found Doullens to be a 'splendid place' where he enjoyed a 'good feed – steak and chips'. On 26 March 1918, Prime Minister Lloyd George and Field Marshal Haig met at the Mairie in Doullens with the French President, Prime Minister and generals to agree how to resist the German Spring Offensive which threatened to split the allied armies and end the war in Germany's favour. The conference appointed General Foch as Supreme Commander of the allied armies and his resolve, 'never surrender', was instrumental in bringing victory in the same year.

18

SERVICE WITH THE LONDON REGIMENT, JUNE 1918–JUNE 1919

Materially, I do not see that victory is possible. Morally, I am certain that we shall gain it.

MARSHAL FERDINAND FOCH ON APPOINTMENT AS COMMANDER-IN-CHIEF
OF THE ALLIED ARMIES, 26 MARCH 1918

George Broadhead joined his new battalion at one of the most critical phases of the war. In spring 1918 the German Army launched repeated assaults along the Western Front and came close to achieving a major breakthrough, which could have brought a disastrous end to the war for the Allies. On 11 April 1918 Field Marshal Haig issued his famous 'backs to the wall' communiqué, stating:

Every position must be held to the last man; there must be no retirement. With our backs to the wall and believing in the justice of our cause each one of us must fight on to the end.

16th Battalion The London Regiment, had served in France since November 1914 and in the spring of 1918 was based in the Arras sector. On 28 and 29 March 1918 the battalion was badly mauled in Operation Mars (the second phase of the German Spring Offensive) while playing a key part in the defence of Arras. The London Regiment was located at Gavrelle, the same village which had seen the decimation of the Bradford Pals in May 1917. The twenty-nine divisions used by the Germans in their Arras offensive greatly outnumbered the sixteen defending divisions but Allied intelligence accurately identified the threat and the Germans failed to make any progress in the face of a well-coordinated defence. The London Regiment suffered more than 200 casualties, of which 150 were listed as 'missing'.

According to the information recorded on the Army Medal Roll, George did not join his new battalion until July and he would have missed the battle at Arras. Given his training as an Orderly Room Sergeant, it is likely that this was his role in the London Regiment but as the London Regiment's War Diary does not mention him by name it is difficult to verify this. Battalion War Diaries rarely gave the names of Other Ranks, in contrast to the routine naming of officers, and the Battalion War Diary is typed so it is not possible to identify his distinctive handwriting.

The battalion stayed in the Arras sector until the end of August 1918 and was billeted at Dainville, a suburb of Arras. Tours of duty in the trenches were carried out at Saint-Laurent-Blangy on the eastern outskirts of the city, only a mile or so from where George's three friends were killed in June 1917. Some time was spent in reserve in the nearby caves at Ronville in the southern suburbs of the city. Throughout the war, the honeycomb of limestone caves under the city had been put to good use by the army for storage and to provide shell-proof accommodation for the troops. At the start of the Arras offensive on 9 April 1917, the caves were used as the launch point for 25,000 of the attackers. However, according to Major J.Q. Henriques, the author of the battalion's war history, the men found the caves to be damp, dark and dirty and life underground had a depressing effect.

On 8 August 1918 the Allies won a tremendous victory to the south at Amiens, which according to the German Army Commander, General Ludendorff was 'the black day of the German Army'. The defeat marked the turning point of the German Spring Offensive and for the rest of the war the German Army was in eastwards retreat towards its own borders. On 21 August 1918 the London Regiment entered the line 8 miles to the southeast of Arras to take part in a major attack on the Hindenburg Line. On 28 and 29 August, in the face of stiff German resistance, the London Regiment attacked the fortified villages of Hendecourt and Bullecourt, and although the battalion suffered around 400 casualties, the attack was successful in overcoming the German defences. After the attack the fighting strength of the battalion was reduced to 200 men and although reinforcements were received, the battalion was never again up to strength with some companies barely mustering fifty men.

The battalion spent the next month in the Bullecourt area absorbing reinforcements before moving 10 miles to the east for an assault on the heavily fortified part of the Hindenburg Line running alongside the Canal du Nord at the villages of Marquion and Sauchy-Cauchy to the south of the city of Douai. The attack was a great success with many prisoners taken. The Battalion War Diary entry for 27 September 1918 reads:

The advance was uniformly successful. Our barrage was excellent and the troops kept well up to it. Such hostile shelling as there was fell in the rear of our Companies. The enemy was mostly found in small trenches in the woods and along the tow path of the canal. As our troops rushed each locality under the barrage, entire groups of Germans came out with their hands up. A large number of prisoners was made in two dugouts near the cemetery. As our platoons were of an average strength of 11 ORs, escorts could not be spared and the prisoners made their way to the rear at the greatest possible speed asking officers they met if an escort could be provided.

Almost 400 prisoners were taken at a cost of around seventy casualties. The contrast with the experience of the battles of 1916 and 1917 could not be more stark. The crossing of the Canal du Nord was a great success. The British troops now faced an enemy who was demoralised and offered little resistance even though he often occupied strong and well prepared positions.

During the assault on the Hindenburg Line, George's younger brother, Tom, who was serving with 7th Battalion East Yorkshire Regiment, won the Military Medal on 26 September 1918 near Gouzeaucourt, just 10 miles to the south of Marquion.

After a period of rest near Arras, the London Regiment took part in the pursuit of the retreating German army and at the beginning of November 1918 was just to the southeast of Valenciennes. On 3 November a patrol led by Sergeant Law entered the village of Saultain unopposed. The men received a warm welcome from the villagers. According to the Battalion War Diary:

The 'D' Company patrol under Sergeant Law had advanced through the village in patrol formation. When the civilians saw it they ran out of their houses cheering. The women seized Sergeant Law's rifle from him and kissed him and brought out coffee for the patrol. Their enthusiasm was tremendous. British and French flags were brought out of the houses and the civilians tried to thrust on the troops all the food and drink they had. The hostile artillery opened on the village but the civilians paid no heed to it or the damage done to their property.

Tom Haslam Broadhead (1898–1979). George's younger brother Tom, a private in 7th Battalion East Yorkshire Regiment, was awarded the Military Medal for bravery in carrying messages under fire in the attack on the Hindenburg Line on 26 September 1918. On that day George was but a few miles away serving with the London Regiment. The pastel portrait is by Otto Nicolai from Munich and is dated 'Lens, France 1919'. Nicolai may have been a German prisoner of war.

The next day the battalion carried out its final attack of the war. In capturing the village of Sebourg the men met heavy machine gun and artillery fire which caused more than 70 casualties. The advance continued and by 11 November the battalion had crossed into Belgium and was billeted in the village of Athis, a few miles to the southwest of Mons. At 6.50 am General Headquarters transmitted the following notice of the Armistice:

Hostilities will cease at 11.00 hours today, November 11th. Troops will stand fast on the line reached at that hour, which will be reported by wire to Advanced GHQ. Defensive precautions will be maintained. There will be no intercourse of any description with the enemy until the receipt of instructions from GHQ.

The London Regiment War Diary entry for this momentous day reads:

Practically every available man engaged on repairing the roads, aided by willing civilians. Armistice signed at 1100 hours. Complete lack of demonstration on the part of the men who carried on as though they were in rest billets. Inhabitants observed in several instances digging up money, clothes etc out of their gardens.

The London Regiment spent the next six months in the Mons area. Numbers were gradually reduced as the men were demobilised and the regiment was finally disbanded in May 1919. On 14 March 1919 a single batch of ten officers and sixty-four other ranks were transferred from the London Regiment to 20th Battalion King's Royal Rifle Corps, which formed part of the army of occupation on the Rhine. George's Discharge Certificate shows service with the KRRC but does not give any detail of dates of which battalion he served in. 20 Battalion KRRC was based at Zons to the south of Cologne but it is not possible to say with certainty that he was with them.

Although the armistice signed at Compiègne on 11 November 1918 brought hostilities to an end, the army needed to retain sufficient troops to man the occupation forces and be able to deal with any resumption of fighting. Not surprisingly, there was considerable criticism from serving soldiers and the public at what seemed inordinate delay in releasing men from active duty, particularly those who had been among the original volunteers. Priority for release was generally given to men from essential industries, such as coal mining, and the longest serving soldiers were often among the last to be discharged. It was not until 21 June 1919 that George was finally demobilised, just one week before the formal peace treaty bringing the war to an end was signed at Versailles, and four years and three months after he had enlisted. An article in the 27 November 1937 edition of the *Batley News* says that at the time of discharge he was serving as an Orderly Room Sergeant in the Army General Headquarters at Rouen. Army GHQ's wartime base had been in the small town of Montreuil but in spring 1919 the headquarters was moved to Rouen which, as a major port, was more suited to handling the administrative and logistical operation of the rundown in Allied troops.

George's Discharge Certificate states that he was transferred to the Army Reserve from the London Regiment and was therefore eligible to be recalled to the colours should it be necessary. His Discharge Certificate shows that he had a fitness category of Bii – less than was necessary for a front line infantry soldier but adequate for garrison or administrative duties. His Army Medal Card shows service with the West Yorkshire Regiment and the London Regiment, and details the award of three medals: the 1915 Star for active service abroad prior to 31 December 1915, the Victory Medal given to all the soldiers in the Imperial Forces, and the British War Medal for all British personnel who served in a theatre of war.

And so ended George Broadhead's military career.

West Yorks and Westminster Rifles cap badges

19

LIFE IN FRANCE,
JUNE 1919 – DECEMBER 1937

There is no reason at all why, in periods as remote from our own as we are ourselves
from the Tudors, the graveyards in France of this Great War shall not remain an
abiding and supreme memorial to the efforts and glory of the British Army,
and the sacrifices made in the great cause.

WINSTON CHURCHILL, SECRETARY OF STATE FOR WAR TO THE
HOUSE OF COMMONS, MAY 1920

Following demobilisation at the end of June 1919, George worked from October 1919 to February 1920 as Chief Clerk in the Army Disposals Office at 36 Rue du Renard in the centre of Rouen, just over a mile from his mother-in-law's house at 8 Rue Traversière where he was living. His leaving reference from the Lieutenant Colonel in charge reads:

Mr G.W. Broadhead has been employed by me as Chief Clerk and Accounts Clerk during the last four months. He has carried out satisfactorily his numerous and responsible duties. He is reliable and painstaking and regular in his attendance. He is leaving my employment through no fault of his own.

George returned to Batley for a short time, working for the Corporation Electricity Department, which he had left when he enlisted. As a respected former employee, Batley Corporation would have been more than willing to find him work but it may not have been easy to bring his new French family to Britain. His wife, Suzanne, was pregnant with their second child, Robert Louis Thomas, who was born on 16 May 1920. There was also the opportunity of work in France and on 7 April 1920,

George left Batley and returned to France to start work with the Imperial War Graves Commission (IWGC) as a 'gardener's labourer' at the St Sever Military Cemetery in Rouen. Given his pre-war and wartime service, working for the IWGC must have been an attractive prospect and would have offered security of employment with a UK-based authority. The good work on which the IWGC was engaged might also have swayed his decision.

The IWGC, which received its Royal Charter in May 1917, was the brainchild of Fabian Ware, the former editor of the *Morning Post* and confidante of a number of influential politicians. The foremost of these was Viscount Alfred Milner, the High Commissioner of South Africa from 1897 to 1901 and member of the War Cabinet. As a civil servant, Ware had worked for Milner in South Africa and had kept in touch with him. When the war came, the forty-five-year-old Ware tried to enlist in the army but was rejected as too old. With Milner's assistance, Ware took command of a British Red Cross Society mobile ambulance unit in France in 1914, taking over a miscellaneous collection of cars and volunteer drivers that made up the Red Cross 'flying unit'. While engaged on this work he saw at first hand the carnage on the battlefields and the haphazard attempts to record the burial places of Allied soldiers, and his unit started to mark and register the graves. Ware's efforts gained official recognition and in March 1915 his unit was incorporated into the British Army and given the title 'Graves Registration Commission'. Ware was awarded the rank of Major. Spurred on by his success, Ware, persuaded the French government to donate land 'in perpetuity' for the burial of Allied soldiers, and in 1917 was able to secure agreement from the UK government to establish the IWGC so that all British and Imperial soldiers could be given equal treatment.

From 1917 to 1920 there was intense and often vitriolic debate about the future role of the IWGC; its funding and the nature and design of the military cemeteries across the world. Ware faced a barrage of competing and conflicting demands from parents who wanted their sons' remains repatriated, those who wanted to choose their own graveside memorials, architects who had strong personal views on the form and style of the cemeteries and memorials, and Imperial preferences expressed by the powerful Dominion representatives who sat on the Commission and government departments concerned about cost. Ware's upbringing as a member of the Plymouth Brethren gave him an inner strength and certainty of purpose, which held him firmly

St Sever Military Cemetery, Rouen. George joined the Imperial War Graves Commission in April 1920 and was based at the St Sever Military Cemetery in Rouen. This large 'concentration cemetery' served the military hospitals located in Rouen during the First World War and contains more than 11,000 graves.

to the principles on which the Commission had been founded. After much controversy, it was finally agreed by Parliament that all the bodies should be buried in the country in which they fell, there should be uniformity in the type of headstone and memorial stones and crosses, and there should be no distinction made between the graves of officers and men. The style of horticulture was to be modelled on the English country garden and in designing the cemeteries and memorials to the missing, the country's pre-eminent architects, Sir Edwin Lutyens, Sir Reginald Blomfield and Sir Herbert Baker, drew heavily on the work and advice of Gertrude Jekyll, the famous garden designer.

With more than 900,000 British and Empire troops buried in Belgium and France, the scale of the task was enormous and, as a construction task, it was the single biggest government project of the inter-war years. The army was given the immediate task of finding and exhuming the bodies. Some were buried where they were found and others were moved to nearby 'concentration' cemeteries, which were usually located on the site of existing military cemeteries. The IWGC was responsible for the construction of the cemeteries and memorials, and by 1921 employed more than 1,300 gardeners in Belgium and France, all of whom had served in the war. Many were housed in IWGC camps or army barracks, often living in very poor conditions in remote parts of the war-devastated French countryside. Charles Longworth, the IWGC's official historian, gives a vivid description of the life of the migrant bands of gardeners who worked along the line of the Western Front:

> In some ways their existence bore similarities to that of the cattle drovers of the pioneering West. Many went out armed, to shoot rabbits, or any other game that lingered on the battlefields, and towards the end of the week their return to camp would be punctuated by often riotous visits to every cafe or estaminet along the way. But these 'travelling circuses' as they were called, did their job, putting as many as 1,375 cemeteries in order in one year.

George was more fortunate in being based at one of the largest war cemeteries in France where continuous employment in one location was possible. In these circumstances gardeners who had married local women were able to live with their families and were generally not called upon to be part of the 'travelling circus'.

The St Sever Military Cemetery in the Rouen suburb of Sotteville-lès-Rouen, where

George started work with the IWGC, is unusual in having two parts to it. During the war Rouen was home to fifteen military and Red Cross hospitals, as well as extensive camps, depots and headquarters, many of which were in the southern suburbs of the city. Soldiers who succumbed to their wounds or illness were initially buried in the city cemetery at St Sever where 3,096 graves are located. By September 1916 more space was needed and an extension to the cemetery, immediately adjacent to the city cemetery, was begun, which, including 328 Second World War burials, eventually housed a further 8,685 graves. The plot layout and large memorial chapel at St Sever were designed by Sir Reginald Blomfield, whose most famous work is the Menin Gate memorial at Ypres. He was also responsible for the design of the Cross of Sacrifice, which is found in the majority of the war cemeteries. With almost 12,000 burials, St Sever is only matched in size by the cemeteries at Passchendaele (Tyne Cot) and Étaples.

To be near to his place of work, George and his family moved from the Levreux family home in the centre of Rouen to Sotteville. The well-appointed house in Rue Henri Boissière, which still stands, is but a five-minute walk from the cemetery. Jacques William, his third son, was born there on 13 June 1925, and his British Consulate birth certificate records George's profession as 'clerk'. This might seem to contradict the IWGC record of his employment as a 'gardener's labourer' and later as 'gardener' but these were IWGC ranks which embraced a range of different duties.

St Sever Cemetery was in the IWGC Arras District and there is evidence from correspondence and photographs that his duties involved visiting other cemeteries in the area. One set of photographs shows him with a group of IWGC workers posing in front of the newly built memorial to the missing of the Battle of Arras at the Faubourg d'Amiens Military Cemetery in Arras. The memorial was unveiled by Viscount Hugh Trenchard in July 1932 and contains the names of the Bradford Pals who were killed in the attack on Gavrelle and Oppy in May 1917 and have no known graves.

George had many friends in France, both expatriates and French people, and enjoyed an active social life, helped no doubt by his fluency in spoken French. He also made regular leave visits to the UK and kept in touch with his old comrades. His private papers include a menu for the 1930 Bradford Pals Comradeship Association annual dinner held at the Market Tavern, Bradford. On the back of the menu is listed the 18th West Yorks football team to play the 16th West Yorks. The names include

Orderly Room Sergeant 'Jackie' Mallett, Regimental Sergeant Major Scott, four officers and on the bench, Sergeant Dickie Bond of Bradford City and England fame.

He maintained contact with members of the Association for a number of years and his papers include an amusing summons to the March 1939 gathering of old comrades from the 18th West Yorks Battalion Headquarters, which is reproduced in part below:

Dear Ancient Perspirations,

As the (married) R.S.M remarked while wending his way down into the cellar for a smoke: 'Life is full of ups and downs.'

This, chaps, is to advise you of a forthcoming UP....

And what, Daddy, was this Battalion Headquarters?
This query took the Committee so much aback that it immediately came overall broody, sat itself down, and forthwith wrote the following poem, lay, ode, glee, shanty, madrigal or doggerel; dashed up to London and pinched a tune right from under the very nose of the Brigade of Guards, and hence:

> *THE BRITISH GRENADIER*
> *Some talk of Alexandria, and of Kantara, too;*
> *Of Oppy and Givenchy, where the mud was just like glue.*
> *But of all the world's great heroes there were none like the few*
> *Who graced the deepest dugout, which was labelled 'B.H.Q'*
>
> *For some did spots of fighting, while others cooked the stew,*
> *But they did all the brain-work (there wasn't much to do)*
> *Yet when it came to supping ale, or scoffing of bergoo,*
> *There was no other section could compete with 'B.H.Q.'*
>
> *Once fought a Scottish Highlander at the Battle of Waterloo,*
> *With wind blew up his bagpipes, as Scottish Highlanders do;*

But nothing like the wind-up that certain swaddies knew.
Who were these chatty Standbacks? The Eighteenth 'B.H.Q.'

If (quoth the Committee, its breath coming in short sharp pants) you want anymore,
please book your seats immediately for the annual love-feast, when additional verses
may (or may not) be perpetrated, assisted by lantern slides, K.R.R.'s, vermorel
sprayers, map references, and huge slabs of four-by-two.

(Note: 'bergoo' porridge; 'swaddies' riflemen; 'chatty' lice; 'KRRs' King's
Regulations; 'vermorel sprayers' device for neutralising chlorine gas; 'four-by-
two' army biscuits or sandwiches)

The invitation is signed by the four 'Honorary Secretaries' of the reunion, one of
which is George's old friend, 'Jackie' Mallett, the Orderly Room Sergeant and another,
the Regimental Sergeant Major, H. Scott. Although the words of the summons
contain much humour, they provide a sharp insight to the conditions of life in the
trenches and its dangers, which had clearly not been left to lie by the members of the
Association.

According to family accounts, the behaviour of George's wife, Suzanne, was often
impulsive and on visits to the UK she attracted much comment for ruffling the
feathers of local market traders whose service she felt was not up to French standards.
My father told me that the divorce came after an incident when '*she had taken after me*
with a gun'. He did not say where the gun came from or what caused her outrage, but
the divorce judgement of June 1936 was granted in his favour and perhaps he was
more sinned against than sinning. A duplicate birth registration certificate for his son,
Jacques, issued in 1947, states that Suzanne remarried in September 1937.

After the divorce, George served a further year with the IWGC at Abbeville. During
the war, the town, which was an important military centre, housed two large general
hospitals and a Red Cross hospital. The hospitals first used the nearby communal
cemetery and as the numbers of burials increased, an extension was created. Sir
Reginald Blomfield, the architect of the St Sever Military Cemetery, designed the
rather austere-looking cemetery which contains 2,500 burials from First World War,
including the graves of nine female workers of the Auxiliary Army Corps who were

killed in an air raid in May 1918. There are also 400 burials from Second World War, of which 200 are from the fighting in May 1940 and the rest mainly of aircrew who were killed in the years that followed.

George's private correspondence describes his work as a member of the Central Committee of the IWGC Wages Staff Association where he helped fight a number of campaigns to improve the pay and pension arrangements of the British staff in France. The main bone of contention seems to be that although all British IWGC staff were deemed to be servants of the Crown, they did not enjoy the same conditions of service enjoyed by UK civil servants serving overseas. Pay of IWGC gardeners was based on equivalent French wages, which were lower than UK wages for the same work, and to add insult to injury, the senior officers of the IWGC in France enjoyed UK rates of pay. The Staff Association lodged an appeal with a UK Industrial Tribunal and the case was about to be heard when George left the employment of the IWGC to return to Britain. The minutes of the Staff Association gave fulsome praise for his efforts in trying to improve conditions for the gardeners.

The letter of reference from his senior officer at the IWGC, dated 4 November 1937, states:

He has proved himself to be a man of exemplary character, good education with an excellent knowledge of office routine…. I can recommend him with confidence for any position of trust, for like all true Yorkshire sportsmen, he will, I am sure, continue his county's prestige for playing the game under all circumstances.

George's private correspondence shows that he was keen to return to Batley and first made enquiries about a gardener's post with the Corporation. An old colleague in the Borough Treasurer's Department alerted him to a vacancy for a clerk in the Housing Department and encouraged him to apply, as Mr Rutter, the Borough Treasurer, was prepared '*to move heaven and earth*' to acquire his services. He had to pay his travel expenses from France but success was assured and he was offered the post. The confirmatory entry in the minutes of the Borough Finance Committee meeting on 25 November reads:

The Chairman and Vice-Chairman reported that they had appointed Mr George

William Broadhead of Batley (at present Senior Clerk, Imperial War Graves Commission in France) as Housing and General Clerk, as from the 13th December proximo at a salary of £156 per annum, rising by two annual increments of £13 per annum to a maximum of £182 per annum.

His appointment was announced in the *Batley News* on 27 November 1937 by the following article:

Post for a 'News' Reader in France

Mr George W. Broadhead a Batley man who served in France during the Great War and who since 1920 has been senior clerk to the Imperial War Graves Commission at Abbeville in France, is recommended by Batley Housing sub-committee for a new position as housing and general clerk in the Borough Treasurer's offices.

Mr Broadhead, who has had the Batley News *sent to him in France regularly since 1920, saw the vacancy advertised in our columns, applied for the position, and has been successful out of seventy applicants. He was formerly employed in the Gas, Electricity and Borough Treasurer's departments of the Corporation.*

Mr Broadhead was born in Halifax Road, Staincliffe and attended Purlwell Board School until at the age of thirteen he started in the Borough Treasurer's offices. Later he worked in the gas and electricity departments. He enlisted in the West Yorks Regiment ('Bradford Pals') early in 1915 and was in Egypt from December 1915 until March 1916. From that date to the end of the war he served in France and on demobilisation held the rank of Orderly Room Sergeant at General Headquarters at Rouen.

Returning to England he took up his clerical duties in the Corporation Electricity Department but returned to France in 1920 on his appointment with the Imperial War Graves Commission.

In pre-war days he played with Staincliffe Cricket Club and in the 1914 season was professional with Great Horton in the Bradford League.

Mr Broadhead, who will take up his new duties on December 13th, is at present staying with his sister, Mrs Samuel Kaye, Leatham Street, Westborough, Dewsbury.

The article does not refer to his divorce or his children and in other respects it is not entirely reliable or complete. For example, it omits reference to his attendance at

Heckmondwike Secondary School and does not give any details of his service with the London Regiment or say much about his service with the IWGC. Nevertheless, it provides interesting background about his pre-war life, work and sporting activities. Mrs Samuel Kaye was his youngest sister Edith (1901–62).

George's eldest son, the twenty-year-old Cecil, who was bi-lingual and had British nationality, came to Britain with his father. He joined the RAF and holding the rank of Flight Sergeant served with the force as a translator until the end of Second World War. Like many other sons of serving IWGC staff, Robert, aged sixteen, joined the IWGC in 1936 but had to leave in February 1938 due to illness. He died in Rouen in late 1938, after being taken from the Hertford British Hospital in Paris against doctor's advice by his mother and grandmother. A letter from the hospital almoner states that he had very serious heart trouble, although I recall my father saying that Robert had died from diphtheria. Jacques, the youngest of his three sons, stayed with his mother in Rouen.

It is clear from letters he received that George was much missed by family and friends in France but, as the threat of another war loomed, he probably felt that he had left at the right time. Many of his colleagues in the IWGC experienced significant hardship when the Germans invaded Belgium and France in May 1940. Some were killed, others were interned or went into hiding, and other escaped. Those who did escape brought very little with them. The Commonwealth War Graves Commission publication, *Remembered*, states that of the 540 British employees in France and Belgium, 206 failed to reach England. A letter to George from Harry Jeal, who had charge of the Varennes Military Cemetery near Albert and was married to a French woman, recounts his 800-mile odyssey in escaping from France. On 4 July 1940 he wrote:

Evacuation order was given at 5.30 pm, 17 May. I managed to get a car and with my family and the owner of the car with her little girl made our way to Yerville, Seine Inferieur. We got there after 32 hours journey, sleeping two nights in the car. The 2nd June we left and made our way to Fougeres, 46 kilometers from Rennes. The IGWC skeleton staff were there. Upon arrival they detailed me to return to Rouen for duty. The wife and all in the car came back with me. On arrival at Bourg Achard I saw the mayor and he refused permission to stay in the commune. We tried another village and had the same reception as everything was reserved for the military. We decided to return to Fougeres. I arrived safely there and reported. They said get the family fixed up and proceed to Rouen. I left 6th June for Rouen by car myself. I was only there 2 days when we had to quit and run back to Fougeres. We left 8th June; at 10.15 the bridges were blown up. All the petrol dumps were destroyed and what a fire! I arrived back at Fougeres 2 days after the 10th June and was in the boat at St Malo, the 13th arriving in England the 14th.

20

SECOND WORLD WAR

Our first line strength did their job remarkably well but the need for greater reserves of trained volunteers would be felt if the area were to suffer sustained raiding. It is up to those not yet enrolled in Civil Defence to take their places among the gallant folk who served us so well the other evening.

GEORGE FREDERICK BOX, MAYOR OF BATLEY, COMMENTING ON THE AIR RAID ON THE TOWN ON 12 DECEMBER 1940 – REPORTED IN THE *BATLEY NEWS* ON 21 DECEMBER 1940

George Broadhead settled quickly to life in Yorkshire and, according to his nephew, Reggie Armitage (the only son of Willie and Lizzie, George's sister, who died in childbirth in 1927), he had no shortage of girlfriends, including a lady in a fur coat from Bradford who collected him in a chauffeur-driven car to go dancing. A letter from a friend in Abbeville asks him: '*Are you still as pure and free hearted as you were in the days gone by? All the nice girls loved our Georgie!*'

My father told me that on the outbreak of war in 1939 he attempted to re-enlist but was rejected on account of age and fitness. That did not prevent him from playing an active part in civil defence and he volunteered for the Auxiliary Fire Service (AFS), carrying out spells of duty in one of its local fire stations. The force was created in 1938 and each local authority was required to establish its own units. They became operational at the start of the war and in 1941 were merged with the regular fire brigades with the new title, National Fire Service. George's AFS membership card was Number 1 which would indicate that not only was he keen to volunteer but he also had a hand in setting up the service in Batley.

He told me of the night of 12 December 1940 when the Luftwaffe bombed the Mount Pleasant and Healey districts of Batley, and one of the observers telephoned the station with the immortal words: '*Ee George! Them's bombs, them is!*' The raid was reported in the *Batley News* on 21 December 1940, describing the death of a soldier and the damage to many buildings. The German aircraft was probably a stray from the large force of 280 enemy planes which attacked Sheffield on 12 December, killing and wounding more than a thousand people and causing enormous damage to homes and industrial premises. As part of his duties in the Corporation Housing Department, George was authorised to act as a Billeting Officer, which under the emergency Defence Regulations gave him the power to requisition accommodation should there be a need.

His correspondence shows that he was active in the national fund-raising schemes, which were directed at buying military equipment and encouraging community participation in the war effort. The 1941 'War Weapons Week' was successful; the people of Batley raised more than £1 million (worth more than £50 million at today's prices), much of which came from the purchase of War Bonds and other savings bonds. Some of the funds went towards aircraft purchases and Batley's coat of arms was displayed on the fuselage of a Mark 1 Spitfire.

George was secretary to the Batley 'Warship Week' Committee, which in the first quarter of 1942 through a variety of local fund-raising events and war savings schemes raised more than £500,000. The sum was sufficient to cover the cost of building a Royal Navy destroyer and the 'Warship Week' scheme allowed towns which had hit their savings target to adopt a ship and exchange commemorative plaques and other memorabilia. The town duly adopted HMS *Badsworth*, a Hunt Class destroyer, and the splendid plaque which followed still holds pride of place in the entrance to Batley Town Hall. The ship itself had an eventful war serving in the Mediterranean, Atlantic and Arctic campaigns. She was mined twice and in 1944 was transferred to the Norwegian Navy and renamed HNoMS *Arendal*. In May 1945 the destroyer was part of the naval escort which took the Crown Prince of Norway to Oslo following the German surrender.

The 'Wings for Victory' week in May 1943 was another success and George was complimented by the Committee Chairman for his unstinting and enthusiastic efforts in organising the processions which were a key part of the week's events. He was also involved in the similar 'Salute the Soldier' campaign, which was launched in Batley on 13 May 1944 by The Princess Royal. The impressive amounts raised by the town in these various savings programmes indicate that the textile industries of Batley were doing well on war orders.

On 16 August 1941 George Broadhead married Margaret Isabelle Fox, a twenty-eight-year-old librarian working in Batley Library. Margaret, my mother, was the second

Margaret Isabelle Fox (1913–83).
Margaret, a twenty-eight-year-old librarian
from Batley, became George's second wife on
16 August 1941. Their children, John and
Janet, were born on 17 June 1945.

child and eldest daughter of Harry James Hubert Fox and his wife, Rachel Hannah Dorsey. The Fox family were among the pioneers of the heavy woollen industry in the West Riding of Yorkshire. Margaret Fox's great-grandfather, William James Richardson Fox, founded the family firm, a textile factory in Bradford Road, Batley, known as Perseverance Mill. He was Mayor of Batley in 1879, a Justice of the Peace and, with other mill owners, was involved in the many civic projects of the rapidly growing Victorian town which received its Charter of Incorporation in 1868. W.J.R. Fox was also a leading member of 'The Zion', the Methodist Church in the centre of Batley and a plaque to his memory is on an inside wall of the church. Following his death in 1920, aged eighty-six, the fortunes of his company declined and Perseverance Mill was closed in 1926, one of the many victims of the post-war depression in the textile industry of the north of England.

His grandson, Harry Fox, continued in business as a felt manufacturer and, despite straitened circumstances, was able to afford the fees to send his children to the local grammar schools. Margaret Fox attended Batley Girls Grammar School, leaving school in 1930 to take up employment in the Young People's department of Batley Public Library. Her appointment, at the princely sum of 12s 6d a week, was of sufficient importance to be reported in the *Batley News*.

The splendid stone-built Carnegie Library is just across the Market Place from the Town Hall where George worked. According to Dorothy Laycock, a librarian colleague of Margaret Fox, George conducted a courtship notable for its determination and reinforced with gifts of food, such as fresh eggs, which were in short supply or subject to wartime rationing. The couple were married at the 'Zion' Methodist Church and the best man was James Henry Shaw who had carried out the very same role in 1918 at George's first marriage in France. Jimmy Shaw had returned to Batley after the war and was employed as a Ratings Officer in the Borough Treasurer's Department. He was also a volunteer telephonist with the Auxiliary Fire Service and perhaps was on duty the night Batley was bombed. He died in 1950.

The local papers carried reports of the marriage and the paragraph below from the *Batley Reporter* contains interesting biographical detail:

Batley Reporter – 23 August 1941

The bridegroom, who is housing assistant for the Batley Corporation served in the last war in France and for many years after the war worked there at the Rouen depot of the Imperial War Graves Commission. He is keenly interested in sport, and while in France played football for Rouen. Since returning to England to take up his present appointment, he has played cricket in the Bradford League and has also assisted Staincliffe. The bride is on the staff at the Batley Public Library and is a prominent member of the Rydings Tennis Club. She is a keen ARP worker, whilst the bridegroom is in the AFS.

I cannot recall my father making any mention of playing football for Rouen but the club's ground, the Stade Robert Diochon, was (and still is) situated immediately adjacent to the St Sever Military Cemetery in the suburb of Sotteville where he worked and lived.

During the 1920s the club had amateur status and it would have been the obvious place to practise his sport.

On 20 June 1943 my mother gave birth to the first of her two sets of twins. One child was stillborn and the other, Michael Fox Broadhead, died the next day. Further tragedy was to follow; eight months after the death of her twins, Margaret's thirty-two-year-old brother, George Hubert Fox, was lost in the sinking of the cruiser, HMS *Penelope* on 18 February 1944. The ship was in transit from Naples to the Anzio beachhead, where it was to carry out shore bombardment duties, when it was torpedoed by the German submarine U-410. Four hundred and seventeen of the crew, including the captain, went down with the ship.

1945 saw the end of six years of war but brought with it prospects for a brighter future in the shape of major social changes in health services, housing and education. For the Broadheads and Foxes, the safe arrival on 17 June 1945 of my twin sister, Janet, and I was also something to celebrate.

The Town Hall, Batley. 'A man of exemplary character … he will, I am sure, continue his county's prestige for playing the game under all circumstances.' The glowing testimonial from a senior member of staff in the Imperial War Graves Commission helped George secure employment at the Town Hall of Batley Borough Council, returning to work which he had left twenty-two years previously.

21

POST-WAR LIFE IN BATLEY

*A housing bombshell was dropped in 1954 when an official government report
showed that Batley had the second worst slum problem, per head of population,
in the whole country. Only Liverpool fared worse.*

THE HISTORY OF BATLEY 1800–1974, BY MALCOLM H. HAIGH

After the war George's career with the Batley Corporation prospered and he became
the town's Housing Manager at a time when the Corporation was carrying out a major
slum clearance programme, with a number of large local authority estates being built
in and around the town. Batley had one of the highest percentages of slum dwellings
in the country and I recall my father's satisfaction at the successful completion of the
rebuilding work and his pride in helping with the naming of new streets and the
encouragement of garden maintenance and tree planting on the kerbsides of the new
roads and streets, a feature of French towns which he admired.

I remember helping him with the meticulous records he kept in carrying out his
duties as an Electoral Registration Officer. He was also active in the local branch of
the National Association of Local Government Officers (NALGO) and was the local
secretary for the Soldiers, Sailors, and Air Force Families' Association (SSAFA). His
work involved frequent contact with Batley councillors but he rarely talked about
politics as such. I only discovered his political leanings when I was working abroad and
asked him to cast a proxy vote for me in the 1970 General Election. He chose to cast my
first ever vote for the Liberal Party, despite my instructions to the contrary!

His enduring passion for sport was met by his membership of Yorkshire County
Cricket Club, which took the whole family and friends to Headingley, Bramall Lane,
Bradford Park Avenue, Scarborough and places beyond. Attendance at Headingley Test
Matches and the annual Scarborough Cricket Festival was compulsory. He was also an

ardent and optimistic follower of Huddersfield Town Association Football Club and was always accompanied by his close friend Austin Whitehead and, from the age of eight, by myself. There were occasional outings to watch Leeds United and Halifax Town, and he and his brother Tom made annual visits to Wembley for the FA and Rugby League Cup Finals.

His love for France and all things French never dimmed and throughout the 1950s and early 1960s he paid annual visits to see his sons – Cecil in Paris and Jacques in Rouen. When we were old enough, Janet and I accompanied our parents.

Cecil's first marriage in August 1939 was to Irene Gardiner from Ruislip where he was stationed in the RAF. The marriage ended in divorce and after the war Cecil returned to France to live in Paris where he ran a company importing and exporting chemical products. His second and third wives were from White Russian families who had fled to France after the Russian Revolution. Zenaide Aronson, known to the family as Zina, who Cecil married in July 1955 at the Dewsbury Register Office, was a ballerina in Diaghilev's Ballets Russes. She was part-owner with her brother of an exclusive Russian restaurant in Montparnasse called the *Dominique*. Irene Bibikoff, his third wife, reputedly came from a family of Russian nobles.

During the war, Jacques fought with the Resistance as a member of the Forces Françaises de l'Interieure (known as FFI). There is a letter from my father to the Secretary for War in Whitehall dated 4 April 1946 supporting Jacques' application to join the British Army (in preference to the French Army) which recounts how he killed a German SS officer and soldier in single-handed combat. In the event, Jacques did not join the army but worked for a short time in Britain as a labourer at an engineering company in nearby Heckmondwike. My father made attempts in 1947 to find Jacques a job with the IWGC in France but the French authorities' insistence that Jacques had French nationality made him ineligible for employment with the IWGC at that time. Jacques returned to France in August 1947.

George resigned, somewhat reluctantly, from Batley Corporation in May 1964 at the age of sixty-nine, complaining that it had needed two people to replace him, one with a degree. The Borough Housing Committee minutes of its meeting on 25 May bear out his complaint in the following entry:

The Borough Treasurer reported on the resignation of Mr George William Broadhead,

Senior Housing Assistant, with effect from 31 May 1964. The Borough Treasurer then submitted proposals for the reorganisation of the housing section as a separate department with the addition of the positions of Housing Manager and Housing Visitor.

Retirement brought an end to fifty-six years of public service of unusual variety and challenge. His remaining years were marked by the deaths in the 1960s in France of his sons, Cecil and Jacques, and I remember his sadness at losing all his French sons. To my knowledge, Cecil's three marriages were childless but Jacques' marriage to Renée Amiot produced nine children, most of whom settled in the Rouen area. In our marriages, my sister and I added another seven grandchildren and my father was certainly not lacking in descendants. In 1965 my mother suffered a severe stroke and my father devoted a large part of his retirement in caring for her with his characteristic determination and devotion until his death on 8 May 1980. My mother's death followed three years later.

Not long before he died, my father spent some time at my sister's house recuperating from an operation. He wandered into the garden to find my 10 year old nephew John playing with his toy soldiers. John asked his grandfather what he remembered about the war and George's first response was: *You don't want to know about that*. John persisted with his question and my father said just one word: *faces* and without further ado turned and walked away.

APPENDIX 1

TIMELINE FOR GEORGE WILLIAM BROADHEAD

19 November 1894	George William Broadhead born at 27 Halifax Road, Batley
1908–15	Employed as a clerk with Batley Corporation
15 March 1915	Enlisted with Second Bradford Pals, 18th West Yorks Regt
6 December 1915	Left Liverpool, bound for Egypt
11 March 1916	Departed Egypt – arrived Marseilles, France
1 July 1916	First day of the Battle of the Somme
19 November 1916	Last day of the Battle of the Somme and twenty-second birthday
25 December 1916	Returned to Batley on leave
3 May 1917	Battle of Arras – severe losses of Bradford Pals
23 June 1917	Arras – death of his 'three best friends'
15 February 1918	Disbandment of the Bradford Pals
6 April 1918	Married Suzanne Marguerite Levreux in Rouen
July 1918	Posted as Sergeant to 16th Battalion The London Regiment
30 October 1918	Cecil George Haslam Broadhead born in Rouen
21 June 1919	Demobilised
7 April 1920	Joined Imperial War Graves Commission (IWGC) in Rouen
16 May 1920	Robert Louis Thomas Broadhead born in Rouen
13 June 1925	Jacques William Broadhead born in Rouen
June 1936	Divorce of George and Suzanne Broadhead
11 December 1937	Resigned from IWGC. Returned to Batley Corporation
16 August 1941	Married Margaret Isabelle Fox at Batley Zion Methodist Church
20 June 1943	Twin boys – one stillborn and Michael Fox Broadhead died the next day
17 June 1945	Twins, Janet and John Broadhead, born
31 May 1964	Retired from Batley Corporation
8 May 1980	George William Broadhead died, aged 85
4 October 1983	Margaret Isabelle Broadhead died, aged 70

APPENDIX 2

SOURCES

The diary of George William Broadhead – 6 December 1915–27 December 1916

Discharge Certificate of George William Broadhead (Army Form Z21)

Medal Card of George William Broadhead

Army Roll of Soldiers Entitled to Victory Medal and British War Medal

Private correspondence of George William Broadhead

Batley Public Library – minutes of Borough Council meetings, 1937 and 1964

Staincliffe Cof E School. *A Short History of the School*. 1869 to 1969 by L. Kemp

Staincliffe Cof E School. Headmaster's Log 1869–1945

Heckmondwike Grammar School. Website: www.heckgrammar.co.uk

Medal Citation and Medal Card for Thomas Haslam Broadhead

NATIONAL ARCHIVES www.nationalarchives.gov.uk

Battalion War Diaries:

    18th Battalion West Yorkshire Regiment WO95/2362/2

    16th Battalion West Yorkshire Regiment WO95/2362/1

    15th Battalion West Yorkshire Regiment WO95/2362/

    1/16th Battalion The London Regiment (Queen's Westminster Rifles) WO95/2963/2

    20th Battalion King's Royal Rifle Corps WO95/1374/4

Publications:

    Battlefront: Somme – published by PRO, 2002

    Battlefront: 1st July 1916 – published by PRO, 1998

COMMONWEALTH WAR GRAVES COMMISSION www.cwgc.org

Military cemeteries and casualty details

Correspondence relating to George Broadhead's employment with the IWGC

IMPERIAL WAR MUSEUM www.iwm.org.uk

Correspondence relating to George Broadhead's diary

Letters from Dr George Boyd McTavish, the Second Bradford Pals Medical Officer

Publications in association with the IWM:

> Burton, Peter. *The Battlefields of the First World War*, Constable, 2005
>
> Burton, Peter. *The Somme*, Constable, 2006
>
> Burton, Peter. *Passchendaele*, Constable, 2007
>
> Burton, Peter. *Arras*, Constable, 2010
>
> Publication in association with the Western Front Association – *Mapping the Front; Somme*
>> – Squares 57C, 57D, 62C, 62D

WESTERN FRONT ASSOCIATION www.westernfrontassociation.com

Stand To! journal

Stand To!, April 2004 edition. Article 'Diary of a Bradford Pal' by J. Broadhead

THE LONDON GAZETTE www.thegazette.co.uk

NEWSPAPERS

Yorkshire Post

Bradford Daily Telegraph

Bradford Weekly Telegraph

Bradford Argos

Batley News

Batley Reporter and Guardian

Dewsbury Reporter

WEBSITES

'The Long Long Trail' www.1914-1918.net

www.ancestry.co.uk

www.findmypast.co.uk including access to census information

OTHER INFORMATION

Christopher Frank – letter dated 23 November 2003 providing details of Leeds and Bradford Pals and other matters.

Family history information for the Broadhead and Fox families.

BIBLIOGRAPHY

Bilton, David. *Hull Pals*, Pen & Sword, 1999

Bilton, David. *Oppy Wood*, Pen & Sword, 2005

Brown, Malcolm, *Somme*, Pan Books, in association with the Imperial War Museum, 1996

Carrington, Charles. *Soldier from the Wars Returning*, Casemate Publishers, 2006

Corns, Catherine and John Hughes-Wolson. *Blindfold and Alone*, Cassell, 2002

Crane, David. *Empires of the Dead*, William Collins, 2013

Dewar, G.A.B. *Sir Douglas Haig's Command*, Constable & Co Ltd, 1922

Duffy, Christopher. *Through German Eyes: the British and the Somme 1916*, Weidenfeld & Nicholson, 2006

Edmonds, Sir James E. *British Official History: Military Operations France and Belgium 1916*, 1932

Farrar-Hockley, General Sir. *The Somme*, Pan Books, 1966

Hart, Peter. *Bloody April*, Cassell, 2006

Hart, Peter. *Somme Success*, Pen & Sword, 2012

Henriques J. Q. *The War History of the 1st Battalion Queen's Westminster Rifles 1914–1918*, London The Medici Society Limited 1923. Reprinted by N&M Press

Horsfall, John and Nigel Cave, *Serre*, Leo Cooper, 1996

Hudson, Ralph N. *The Bradford Pals*, Bradford Libraries, 1998

Hughes, Kathryn. *Great War Britain Bradford Remembering 1914–18*, The History Press, 2015

Johnson, Malcolm K. (ed.) *Miners' Battalion (12th Pioneer KOYLI)*, Pen & Sword, 2017

Lais, Otto. *Experiences of Baden Soldiers at the Front*, G. Braun Karlsruhe, 1935

Liddle, Peter. *The Worst Ordeal*, Leo Cooper, 1994

Mace, Martin and John Grehan. *Slaughter on the Somme 1 July 1916*, Pen & Sword, 2013

Masefield, John. *The Old Front Line*, Pen & Sword, 2006

Messenger, Charles. *Call to Arms. The British Army 1914–1918*, Weidenfeld & Nicholson, 2005

Middlebrook, Michael. *The First Day On The Somme*, Classic Penguin, 2001

Middlebrook, Martin and Mary. *The Somme Battlefields*, Penguin Books, 1994

Nicholls, Jonathan. *Cheerful Sacrifice*, The Battle of Arras, Leo Cooper, 1993

Oldham, Peter. *The Hindenburg Line*, Leo Cooper, 2000

Philpott, William. *Bloody Victory*, Little, Brown, 2009

Raw, David. *Bradford Pals*, Pen & Sword, 2005 *[Note: all the quotes in this book attributed to CQMS Parker should be to George William Broadhead. The author apologises for his error.]*

Rogerson, Sidney. *Twelve Days on the Somme*, Frontline Books, 2006

Stamp, Gavin. *The Memorial to the Missing of the Somme*, Profile Books, 2006

Summers, Julie. *Remembered: The History of the Commonwealth War Graves Commission*, Merrell, 2007

Tallett, Kyle and Trevor Tasker, *Gavrelle*, Leo Cooper, 2000

Wilkinson, Roni. *The Pals on the Somme 1916*, Pen & Sword, 2006

Wood, Stephen. *The Leeds Pals*, Amberley Publishing, 2014

Woods, Mike and Patricia Platts. *Bradford in the Great War*, Sutton Publishing, 2007

Wyrall, Everard. *The West Yorkshire Regiment In The War 1914–1918*, Volumes 1 and 2, Naval & Military Press

INDEX